WHAT
Girls
KNOW

by

NEESHA MEMINGER

Ignite

See It Be It Productions

For information about this title, please contact
See It Be It Productions
info@seeitbeit.com
NeeshaMeminger.com

10 9 8 7 6 5 4 3 2 1
Meminger, Neesha
What Girls Know / Neesha Dosanjh Meminger.—1st ed.
Summary: A group of teen girls heal from the emotional and psychological impacts of sexual assault and childhood sexual abuse through art, creative expression, meaningful connection with others, and mobilizing for social justice.

Library of Congress Control Number: 2019904904
1st ed. ISBN 978-0-983-1583-4-9 (paperback)
ISBN 978-0-983-1583-5-6 (eBook)

Other Books by Neesha Meminger

Shine, Coconut Moon

Jazz In Love

Into the Wise Dark

This book is for Barbara, my fairy godmother, who always told me my writing was the answer.

Acknowledgements

What Girls Know arrived after many years of not writing. After my marriage ended, my creative well was completely dry, and there seemed to be no indication that it would ever fill again.

But it did, and I have many people to thank. First and foremost, Cori Worchell, Amy and Jeff Carr, Bix and Joe, Zetta, Zohra, Sarah McCarry, and Melinda Garrick; all folks who stepped in to help me pick up the pieces after the life I'd thought was stable began to crumble beneath me.

Of course, my parents, brothers, and Kinder and Jeet, who were constantly at my side with words, food, comfort, and practical support all the way through.

I would never have been able to write this story if it hadn't been for the art therapy and trauma groups I participated in as I worked through the wounds that would, in the end, be shaped into the words on these pages. I am eternally grateful to the following: the YWCA for making art therapy groups free for women who've experienced violence; all of the groups at the Women's College Hospital in Toronto for women recovering from childhood abuse, neglect, and violence; Lesley Hughes for embodying love in a manner so similar to the character of Cathy in this book.

Thank you, also, to the women at Breakthrough: Carol Barrett, Suzanne, and Maria Teresa. Your kindness, tenderness, and careful curiosity unlocked parts of my heart. I am also grateful for the women I've been lucky enough to meet, who are engaged in creative art therapies; I believe in the power of the arts, to heal and create change, more passionately than ever.

I have tremendous gratitude for the mental health programs that allowed me access to therapy throughout my teen and adult years. Arts and mental health resources have always been under siege, but they are especially so now. It has never been more important to fight clawbacks and save the gains we've made. These arts and mental health programs are the tools that empower us. Anything that empowers vulnerable people to fight on their own behalf, or to advocate for self-agency, is a threat to existing power structures and systemic control, yet it is critical to our survival, not just individually, but as a planet.

A deep and heartfelt thank you to Toni. If you're reading this, you know exactly who you are.

Foreword

Dear Reader,

The following is a story about my healing journey from the effects of childhood sexual abuse within a religious setting. Like Audre Lorde's "biomythography," this is a fictionalized memoir of my actual journey. But memory is a funny thing, and trauma doesn't always come out like a documentary film. It makes itself known in images, fragments, whispers while you're half asleep, and disjointed words and phrases. Everything is cloaked in the fear, shame, and confusion that accompany moments of shattering; moments when the psyche is thrust abruptly into survival mode.

My memory of the abuse, however, is clear and sharp. At times, I was watching myself from afar, from outside of my body, as if it were happening to someone else. Numerous studies have shown that children do, in fact, have out-of-body experiences when they are traumatized. Children have accurately described, in great detail, events and people in locations sometimes far removed from where the trauma was occurring.

And in the aftermath, there is a tremendous pull for survivors to go back and retrieve the parts of soul and psyche that were broken and left behind. Parts that felt stolen or snatched away. When I first felt that pull, I was fifteen; nine years after the abuse. That was when I began therapy—individually, in groups, and through creativity.

After decades of psychotherapy in different modalities, I have an unshakeable faith in the power of healing through art. I am especially, and perpetually, fascinated with the intersection where art, healing, and spirituality merge.

This story came after my divorce which, unexpectedly, placed my feet on the path to a deeper kind of healing than anything I'd ever known. Because of all the years I'd spent reflecting on and examining my past, I thought I was good. All healed. I was a well-functioning, successful, happy adult. I was married, my children were healthy and confident, and my novels were being published by enthusiastic publishers. I was on my way to the life I'd dreamt of, and recorded in my journals since I was 12-years-old.

The breakup of my marriage shook the foundations of my entire belief system. The work I'd done to heal myself until then had been Herculean, but I realized there was still more to be done. I will never forget what my mother said when I told her my marriage was over. "Lies are like rats, honey. If you see one in the house, you know there are a hundred more in the walls, and you have to bomb the entire place."

I realized then that my marriage had been constructed on careful lies and, suddenly, I was face to face with the trauma that had allowed me to walk into a den of deceit, believing it to be truth. My early trauma was saying "LOOK AT ME".

So, I went back to my roots: therapy, writing for process rather than product, activism, healing through art, and developing connections through groups and community.

I created a lot of art in that time. I did a lot of wondering if I was going to make it. I sobbed, screamed, and went numb. But I kept picking up that thread that connected me to my truest self. My daughters are a huge part of what got me through, but so was this little glowing ember inside me, the tiniest barely-there flame that just kept on flickering.

This book is what came out of that journey. I wanted to put it out there, because I know there are readers who will need these words. Readers who needed them yesterday, and last year, and decades ago. I was not alone in that temple. And sexual abuse in houses of worship is a bigger problem than most people realize.

This book is not meant to be Poetry, or "high art"; it is a love poem to those who have struggled to connect to that wispy, spidery, sometimes elusive thread of hope. Especially if that hope was stamped out early on.

Putting this experience into the world has been the most courageous step I've taken in breaking the silence around what happened. I worried about the whatabout-ers and the ya-but-

ers. *Those who wonder why survivors don't speak up sooner. My answer to them is: Do your research on childhood trauma. And my other answer is: I did speak up. Most of us do. Our bodies and behaviors scream* I was hurt *in so many ways that have become normalized in our fractured and traumatized world. We are living on a planet that is hollering* I have been hurt *so loudly, its shuddering spasms are all around us, and those of us who recognize the cries feel the urgency, like never before, to do something. To speak up. To protect the vulnerable and sacred.*

I spoke up as soon as I had words for my body parts and understood what had happened to me. I told. I told at thirteen. At fifteen. And again at seventeen. And twenty-one, and thirty-five, and again at forty-two. And now. I am telling again, now.

I worried about airing the dirty laundry of my family, my community, my people. *Especially now, when Black, Brown, Indigenous, and POC bodies are under siege in a world increasingly becoming polarized. But being a survivor of childhood sexual abuse by trusted religious leaders is a whole other beast. It is beyond race, ethnicity, and culture. It puts me right alongside the child victims of the Catholic Church, the Southern Baptist Church in the U.S., and the Anglican Church in the U.K.*

I'm not saying what happened to me is an epidemic in Sikhism. I don't know to what extent or how often it occurs, because I doubt it has been, or would ever be, reported. I do know some of my cousins and friends had similar experiences, but never came forward and likely never will. And I believe child-hood sexual abuse in a religious context is an obvious out-growth of a corrupt, twisted, and dying system that is based on the unquestioned power of patriarchy, misogyny, capital-ism, and imperialism. This is not unique to any one religion. It is a global epidemic that is killing off the very planet that sustains us.

Childhood sexual abuse attacks you at your core. Your hope, your faith. And it grooms you to be the perfect quiet victim. It makes you think you did something to bring it on. For the longest time, I thought there was something about my body – at the age of six, even – that made men do certain things. That, perhaps, there was something especially wrong or dirty about me and because of it men lost control . . . forgot how to behave like adults. I mean, here were these holy men, men everyone trusted and revered and loved. The problem had to be me, right?

Hope is fragile, and children are incredibly, incredibly *vul-nerable. I didn't understand that until I worked with a very special therapist in my forties, who was partly the inspiration for the therapist in this book. She would say it in every single session. "Neesha, children are so unbelievably,* incredibly *vul-nerable!" She would say this to me with her entire body, trying to impress upon me that I was a child at the time of the abuse, completely dependent on the adults around me to survive. She had worked with actual children who'd been raped. She knew what children at that age look like. What words they know. How small their hands, fingers, legs. How trusting they are. How desperate to be loved, and how quick to offer love.*

I wrote this story as a YA novel-in-verse because that is how it came out. That is how it wanted to be told. The words flowed to me from outside of myself, from the past, from an eternal present . . . I'm not sure. But they came to me from a place of truth, trying to shape the events of my life into a useful narrative.

I was fifteen, depressed and suicidal, and incredibly alone when I first found a therapist. I was desperate to speak my truth somewhere, to someone who would listen. And that was the beginning of my healing journey. Perhaps that's what draws me to the YA genre. Those years are so tumultuous, definitive, urgent. We've lost so many of our young during these young adult years, when their bodies and behaviors are loudly hollering, but they don't have the words, guidance, or a path to healing.

Packed into this story is all my love for my fellow humans who have been sexually abused as children and survived to tell about it, as well as those we've lost. This story, clunky in parts, and imperfectly told in others, is the gift I've spent my entire life crafting. I hope it is useful.

PART ONE

What

Happened

Chapter One

What happened

There's this thing
that happens
when a child
is sexually abused
by holy men

trust is betrayed
but something else
more shattering
that reaches across
inviolable boundaries

alters irreversibly
the timespace settings
flings razor wire
back through generations
impacting all future iterations

trust is betrayed
but the larger version of it
the truer version of it . . .
faith
is shredded irreparably

when the life force
is defiled
in the house of god
how do I find my faith again?

Our story

This story, the one I am going to tell you
is about me
it is my story

and it is also not my story; ancient
it is about us
our story

there are things that happen to me in it
but these things
are also all things

my body was violated
by holy men
in a house of god

as the earth body,
raped repeatedly
before our eyes

holy men devour tender green shoots
dew dropped beginnings
turning to find the sun

men who were empty
voids grasping
for something to fill

hollow spirits
preaching
words of god

it was not theirs
to claim
not theirs

my wails in those rooms
and then my silence
as I imploded

is the same
shattering cries
of water protectors

it is the wails of children
torn from mothers' arms
after walking a thousand miles

this is my story
of healing
from being broken

by holy men
in the house
of god

but it is your story, too
our story
we are still writing it, together

What the blind woman saw

The only person to ever truly
see me

was an old blind woman

she would trace my features
marveling at the swoops
of my eyes, the flare of my nostrils

everything was royal
I had a majestic nose
a regal chin
queenly cheekbones

she adored me, told me
not to forget I was perfect, precious

worth more than anything
my mother could possibly own

I had no idea then
how important it would be
for my body to know
those words

that I would never hear anything
like them again
not from my mother, not from anyone
that everything around me would tell me otherwise

and that once we left India
I would never see this woman again,
the only person who would ever see me
the only person to ever love me so thoroughly

that I would be torn from everything
including my own self
the moment I left the heat and song of India behind
the moment I left her protective arms behind

and I would never return
and she would die begging anyone
to bring me back just one more time
so she could see me again

this is that story . . .

Before

*The blind old woman
traced the girl's face
mapping a terrain
trying to pin it down
to keep it
from flying away
forever*

*fingers hovering, trembling
the woman whispered
"this child's face will disappear
like their promises to return"*

*the old woman wanted to tell the girl,
her beloved Anjal –
a grandchild she'd never had –
all the stories . . .
of serpents, of magic,
and especially, of power*

*stories that needed to be shared
stories that would help the girl,
and many girls after*

but the old woman knew
they needed to leave
the winds had changed

Anjal...her very name
meant free flowing wind

she hadn't wanted to believe
even here, this land of
Sufis and saints
gurus and Budhas
myths and Mahabharatha,
even here
men would fall prey
to their own fears

it was time

the girl's destiny was on the other side
of a turbulent and opaque sea

if the woman told her now,
the girl would be frightened
and they were leaving in the morning

"your mother is a fool"
the old woman muttered into the emptiness
"she believes the lies of men
"holds their untruths like jewels to her chest"

perhaps this was how it was meant to be . . .
perhaps the girl was meant never to know

perhaps this girlchild's face
so beloved
beneath her gnarled fingertips . . .
was meant to vanish from her touch
forever

A cave with beasts

The girl gripped her father's hand

he spoke with the temple men
turbaned, swords hanging at their hips
smiling beards
hands folded in greeting
the temple quiet
holy

her father was no longer turbaned
no longer had a beard

it was not safe in the new country
for men to have beards and turbans
Anji had heard the grownups talking
had seen it on the news
before her father snapped the tv off

but here, in the temple
it was okay
to have the faith of your ancestors
the faith they fought and died for

the temple
was dark and cool and quiet
reminding her of a cave
with bats,
or the kind of beasts
with giant jaws lived in

she moved closer to her father's legs

~ * ~

It was so nice to speak the language of home

to speak with men, laugh with them
to be understood by good, solid, decent men
from home

he crouched down,
"don't make trouble, doll
"be a good girl
"I will pick you up after work
"I won't be long"

he peeled her off his leg
wrenched his pants free of her fists

and then, steeling his ears to her cries
erasing the image of her crumpled face
the betrayal shining in her eyes
he marched into the blistering wind
of the new country

he did not know the new words
or all of the new laws
at work he would find his lunch gone
replaced with garbage – actual garbage
someone had picked out of the can in the hallway

some nights they followed him
to the bus stop
with threats, warnings
pushing, shoving
go home

don't escalate,
he would repeat in his head
let it roll off
it's nothing

and he would swallow the
bitter stone of shame
humiliation powerlessness

he would never be welcome
maybe
but his children . . .
they would be safe
here, they would have opportunity
to become something
do great things

he could face anything
knowing they were safe
and right now they were

in the hands of holy men
men of god
men from home

his little girl
would hear familiar words
eat foods she knew
surrounded by smells
reminding her of the home
she still expected to go back to

he didn't have the heart
to tell her
they would never return

but for now
she would be in god's house
with god's word

she would be
safe

A boy named River

There is a boy
his name is River
a perfect name for a perfect boy

he flows cool
and laps gentle
softly shapes the world around him

there is something about him that
tugs at her memory
but when she turns
to find it
it skittles away

his smile
the way he moves
the way his hawk eyes
zero in

a cat in a jungle

she can't put her finger on it
but doesn't need to because her breath
. . . it leaves her body when he's near

because her insides want to flee
when he's near
want to climb up and out of her skin
and her heart stops
and separates from everything around it
and then she is under water

she doesn't remember her name
where she is
who she is
when he is near

A good girl

Something has happened to Anji
she has always helped

taken care of her little brother
translated English for her parents
explained why girls at school
shave their legs and armpits
and she wants to, too

she has learned to
sweeten the sound of her voice
too deep for a girl
stop dancing singing laughing too loud

her hair is tied back
not loose
not wild

she has always been smart
never a problem

because there are enough problems
her parents are working hard
in a new country
that wants them
and doesn't want them
at the same time

come here and work
go home, you don't belong here

Anji is a good girl
because things are hard enough

River has cut through her
creating a deep gash
where before there was ice
there is movement now
where everything was frozen

and now something
is whispering
like a serpent hissing
waking rising swaying
fire water ripping
cutting her open

Warmth, at last

Come to my place, he says
my parents aren't home
and something inside her stirs
something old
ancient
something remembered

I have calculus, she says
with Mr. Shah

so? cut class
he moves closer and whispers
kiss me

her insides fly out of her skin
and there it is
the remembered thing
only she can't see it

it's a remembered thing
inside her skin
in the cells there

and the kiss
it burns down
the core of her
cuts her on all sides
it is the remembered thing
that she can't see

that kiss
she would live in it forever . . .

it is the sun it is life it is everything

like a peony
lifting her face to the sun
she follows his light
his warmth

Take me away

This kiss feels like
being in the arms of a lover
who was never meant to have you

the only sun
in a frozen place
she needs more
       desperately more

there are answers there
something hidden
under frozen depths
precious discarded secrets
shards of a former self

tattered skin left behind
remainders of a violent past

her heart stops when
she sees him
then pounds furiously

a fist against a closed door

Riv . . .
his name is a prayer
in a temple
where children are safe
from foreign terrors

where they are reminded of home
under the care of pious men
in a house of god

Unfreezing

So this is what it feels like
doesn't hurt
doesn't feel good
nothing
because she's not there

nothing matters now
but Riv

and the sharpness
that wakes her
unfreezes her
jolts her back into living
whenever she's with him

this girl at school, Toni, cuts her skin
everyone knows it
and Anji has seen the marks
when they walk to school together

she doesn't know Toni that well
but she likes her
Toni lives a couple of blocks
away and they walk the same route
to school a couple of mornings a week

Toni doesn't talk much
but when she does, it's about
big world things
governments and capitalism
things Anji doesn't think much about

Toni doesn't bug
Anji about Riv
Anji knows people are whispering
talking to her with fake faces
trying to figure things out
but not Toni
Toni gets it

some people's marks
are on the outside
but cutting works the same
on the inside

Chapter Two

Neesha Meminger

All Wrong

Something's wrong
Anji knows it
but she doesn't know what
. . . what happened

her dreams are of trains
going off the tracks

she feels like she's slipping
down a mountain
no one around to see
to hear

nothing to grasp
nowhere to land
no way
to stop it

crying all the time
when no one is around

darkness seeping into
her pores all the time
smothering her breath

she doesn't speak much anymore
doesn't raise her hand in school
doesn't care about classes

her straight A's are now
scattered F's

something's wrong
but she doesn't know
how to fix it

she wants eyes
like the sun
to land on her
to *see* her

but she is sinking
in a river of darkness
and does not know
what happened

Melting

Riv has other girls
Anji knows this
doesn't care
she needs this and can't explain why
she lies to her parents to be with him
she lets him do whatever he wants

he takes her money
when she's not looking
and it doesn't matter

when he walks past her
like he's never met her
it doesn't matter

he moves through her
down the center of her
scraping along the sides of the gash
a giant glacier creating friction
sparks
fire and ice
down the center

when she's not around him
she feels the deadness inside
a shell of emptiness

she's a squeeze-small
make-things-easy
don't-make-trouble
kind of girl
and she's
doing everything wrong

Eruptions

Volcanoes erupt without warning
they look quiet on the outside
dead, even
sometimes for hundreds of years

but when the lava inside
gets hot enough
they erupt

and sometimes they wipe out
entire civilizations

there is a simmering
under the deadness inside

Anji cuts classes sometimes
and writes poetry in her journal
doodles things
and something about this makes her restless

she wanders the empty halls
out of sight and in the shadows
under the stairs and in vacant corners

and something is simmering
words, elbowing their way up
trying to make it onto the page

a kind of lava wants to flow
hot black ink onto the page
erupting spewing sputtering
desperate to be seen
in doodles or swirls or words
anything

she wanders
searching
writing
drawing her own river

Guidance

They said at all the assemblies
that students can go to a guidance counselor
if they ever need to

Anji doesn't know if this will help
but she is failing everything
and doesn't know why
she is in the halls all day
leaving classes to "go to the bathroom"
and then just not returning

when she writes
the words that come out
sometimes scare her

so she takes a deep breath
and walks into the Guidance office

Ms. Murphy is the counselor
she has eyes that crinkle at the corners
skin that looks like a soft leather sofa

why haven't you been going to your classes?
she asks

I've been sick

Ms. Murphy nods
is quiet for a moment

and prods a bit
and then a bit more

until tears prick Anji's eyes
and then stream down her face

the words are stuck in her mouth
like sharp triangles
pinching and piercing
soft insides

the counselor's questions
jab her inside
the gentleness of her tone hurts
the concern in her eyes tears at her

Anji wants to flee
wonders why she ever thought this was a good idea

but she wants to stay too

Ms. Murphy's questions
feel like sandpaper against tender skin
but she is listening
leaning forward in her chair
her eyes on nothing else
but Anji's face

Anji wants to leap
into those eyes
and run screaming from the office
at the same time

she wants to tell her something
but she doesn't know what
doesn't know how

this counselor's kindness
is unraveling

Anji reaches into her backpack
opens her journal with trembling fingers
and slides it toward Ms. Murphy

this is it
her molten lava on paper
on the desk
under Ms. Murphy's unsettling eyes

Anji feels sick to her stomach
but stays put
what is the alternative?
she asks herself
keep wandering the halls?
fail everything?
her parents would find out
and that is even worse

Ms. Murphy reads
slowly and carefully
turning pages like she's under water
and Anji feels like
she is going to pass out

then, Ms. Murphy closes the journal
and turns toward Anji
she looks at her like it is just
the two of them on the planet

this is so important
she says, handing the journal back
so valuable

valuable
important
words that reverberate in Anji's mind

I'm so glad you came to talk to me,
she says
I would love to see more of your work
why don't you come back tomorrow?

and Anji does
she looks forward to the days
Ms. Murphy is in
so she can show her
her words and doodles

Chapter Three

The wounded wound

Riv is getting worse
there is a gash down his center too
but Anji doesn't know its shape its color
maybe it's his dad
whose hands are always fists

maybe it's his mom
who's always hiding bruises
or his sister
who doesn't ever talk

Anji doesn't know what it is
but she wants to make it better

even when he flirts with other girls in front of her
even when he yells at her
even when he smokes her up
gets her so high she doesn't remember her name
and then leaves her on the side of the road
to walk home by herself

even when he takes her to neighborhoods
where you have to wait for the shooting to stop
before you can run out to the car

even then

he doesn't know it's there, maybe
this deep gash
but Anji sees him spinning
and knows that feeling

knows what it's like to spin
to be dead but alive
there but not there

he plays basketball and laughs and jokes . . .
like everything is okay
and Anji knows that too

she watches him and waits
all she needs is for him to light that spark again
to give her something
just one thing anything
to stay for

kisses and body heat
a touch from someone anyone
something that feels like the sun
warmth

she flirts with other boys too
words fading to nothing
but her body speaking
a language they understand

Riv acts like he doesn't care
and maybe he really doesn't

other boys touch her
in the same places he does
but they are not him
they don't rip her down the center
and open her up

don't warm her the way he does
don't tug at that something
in her muscles
an old memory
quiet but alive

dormant volcano

they don't do that
the other boys
so she feels nothing
still dead and dying
desperate
to breathe and live

she waits clawing
at her insides until he is with her
again soothing
bandage on an open wound

and she can tilt her face
like a many petaled peony

but he is in trouble
and she doesn't know what kind
it's the kind that has police officers
at the school
the kind that has the school calling his parents
and sending email blasts
to all other parents
some of you may have noticed police cruisers
no cause for alarm, folks

but this is the kind of trouble
that has him so high
he stays slumped on a curb
outside behind his work for hours
Anji sitting next to him

she wants to hold him
make him come alive
take away whatever makes him
smoke everything away

she knows that thing
that makes you run and hide
from your own body
flying out or running deep inside

she holds his face
between her hands
plants salty kisses
he will never know were there

he slurs out a sentence
something about his father
something about his sister
Anji's lips tremble
tears that never come for her
come for him

she holds his head against her chest
sits with him for a long time

A New Beginning

You've been coming to see me,
Ms. Murphy says,
for about six weeks now, Anji

you can keep coming
as long as you'd like
I will always make time for you
and I always want to see your writing

Anji is not liking the feeling she's getting
like a goodbye is about to round the corner

but some of the things you're uncovering
through your writing and art
are things I think you might want to talk about
with someone who is more qualified than I am
and can help you better

Anji's throat is tight
she looks forward to seeing Ms. Murphy
she writes because she knows someone
will see her words
the things she can't say

what do you mean?
she asks

Ms. Murphy inhales deeply
some of the things you're writing about, sweetie
are descriptions of abuse and trauma

something sinks inside Anji
no, she says,
there's been no trauma

Ms. Murphy's face has gone
so soft and tender
it makes Anji want to scream
but she whispers, *no*

her hands flutter
to the sides of her face
to hold everything in

I just want . . .
just want to keep seeing you
to keep . . . showing you what I'm writing

Ms. Murphy's hand
goes to her own heart
oh, love
she says,
I know
you can keep doing that,
she says softly
and then scribbles something
down on a post-it

take this number,
she says,
and call them
it's so important
that you get the support you need
and you know that,
she adds,
because you sought me out
and trusted me

her eyes are so warm
her face so soft and caring

Anji takes the post-it
maybe she will call

she wonders
if it's always the people
who are hurt
who have to reach out
to find a branch to grab onto
to save themselves

Witness

Sometimes
when Anji looks
into Riv's eyes
a memory unfurls

a tendril, stretching
taking root
not yet at the surface,
but growing . . .

some of the men play games
with the children
some of the games are fun
some are not

the games with girls
are different
than the games with boys

some of the children
are there with siblings
Anji is there with her brother, Surjit

he is her only ally
when their parents drop them off
each morning

Neesha Meminger

Surjit sees everything
remembers everything

he knows what happens
to Anji during nap times
but he's little
he can't do anything
but cry

they don't do the same things
to him
he is little, only three
and everything scares him
they think it's funny
when he's scared
when he runs and hides
behind Anji

they scare him more
and laugh
because it's funny
to see a little boy
run scared by holy men

when some things happen
Surjit goes deep inside
and Anji can't get him back again

then her only ally
the only one who hasn't left her
is gone
and she's alone again

some nights
she wakes up shouting
"don't go!"
to dreams of slammed doors
then, dark emptiness envelopes her
and she steadies her breathing
knowing no one is coming

and that is okay
because sometimes
knowing no one is coming
is better in the darkness

For love

So she does it

after dialing and hanging up
a thousand times
seeing the unasked question
in Ms. Murphy's eyes
a thousand times

she finally calls the number

part of her is excited
could it be that there is
happiness out there?

is there some way to get there?

maybe someone at this place
has some answers

part of her is terrified
like she is telling things
she's not supposed to

taking the soft private
of her family's hurt
and paging through it in public

but she does it
she calls

she makes an appointment
with a counselor named Cathy
during her spare period

she thinks about canceling
the appointment all day
and during the entire bus ride
to the Youth Clinic

and here she is now, with Cathy
Cathy with a soft voice
and skin that looks like iced tea
in the summer
concerned eyes like Ms. Murphy's

for the first few visits
there is a lot of
Cathy filling out forms
and taking notes

family history,
she says

where did you move to?
why did you move?
and where to after that?
siblings?
tell me about mom and dad

Anji answers
like she does at school
on tests
it's easy
just words
facts
first this happened
then this
and then this next thing

after a few sessions,
Cathy starts asking different questions
like, what about your body?

and then Anji has no
answers
no words at all
sometimes she doesn't
even understand Cathy's

she gets confused
and sometimes feels like
she's floating

those times,
Cathy asks where she is
it's confusing to Anji
I'm here, she says

Cathy says, tell me what's going on
in your body
and Anji tries to shape
the floatiness
the scatteredness
into words

everything flies away
like a frightened flock of birds

Cathy nods
and reaches for the big rock she keeps
on her table
hold it, she says
feel its shape
what temperature is it?
how heavy does it feel?
is it smooth or rough . . . ?

Anji can answer
these questions
she knows the words
for these
and it brings her back
it lands her back in her body

and then sometimes
she can only cry
still no words
but lots of tears

and that's when she's not nauseous
when her body doesn't feel
like it wants to throw
everything up

when all the moments
from the past aren't
making a loud clanging
in her belly

when it quiets down
and melts inside

then there are tears

No one else

You okay?
Toni asks, one day
on the way to school

Anji nods,
swallowing hard
pushing all the words down

you don't look okay,
Toni says
you actually look really not okay

Anji glances at Toni
she wants to say,
can I trust you?

she wants to say,
I want to trust you
but she doesn't

even with the scars
on her arms
Toni would never understand

they have nothing in common
no one could possibly understand

Anji has never felt more alone

Chapter Four

Telling

Anji is at her job
flashing lights and sirens
red and white and howling
there's been a robbery

Riv took all the money out of the cash register
everything all the fifties twenties tens fives singles
everything
and left with his car full of friends
during Anji's shift

was there a girl in the car?
was Julie somethingorother in there?

the cops are looking at Anji
did you take it?
they ask

she shakes her head
but they are in her face
if you didn't take it, who did?

the store manager is staring at Anji
she knows
she has seen Anji with Riv before
the store manager hates guys like Riv
be careful of him, she's said to Anji

where is the money?
the officer repeats
who took it?
if it was you
you will have to repay it
and you will be charged with a crime

your parents will be informed

her eyes widen
don't make any trouble

she is cornered
in a dark room
he slides a notepad toward her

write down everything you know
about the person who took the money

she begins writing
slow and shaky at first
and then everything piles out
jagged and awkward
sharp and unwieldy
she looks down and there are a lot of words

afterward she's trembling

she just told on Riv

she put cold hard words
around razor sharp incisors

told a secret
his secret her secret
that will make things bad
that will make Riv hate her forever

Trouble

Riv is behind bars
his mother snarls
at Anji
this is all your fault

his sister whispers *whore*
every time she passes
in the halls at school
and something deep inside Anji
agrees with her

she has made a lot of trouble
she has broken the rules
and told on people

she has always been smart
never a problem

but something is simmering

words, elbowing their way up
trying to make their way out

a kind of lava wants to flow
hot black and red

erupting spewing sputtering
desperate to be seen

even if it means
she will betray everyone

to save something
much more important

Neesha Meminger

Curse and prayer

The cops explain to her parents
that Anji was the victim
she'd done nothing wrong
that she was required to stay
at the police station
to write out a victim's statement
and that she did the right thing
by telling the truth

Anji's parents nod and listen
and nod some more
they thank the officers
shake their hands

Anji knows inside they are humiliated
their daughter has arrived home
in the middle of the night in a police car
for the entire neighborhood to see

her mother's face is frightening
her father's face is vacant

the cops leave

Anji walks past her mother
to go up the stairs to her room
and her mother punches her
in the middle of her back

all the breath leaves Anji's body
she lays sprawled on the stairs for a long time
trying to breathe

this is what we work so hard for?
this?? so you can shame us?
do you know what people will say?

her parents are disgusted
they leave her on the stairs
don't even look back

how could she behave like this?
what must the neighbors be thinking?

this is why girls are a curse
they bring shame and dishonor
they destroy families

Anji sits up slowly
wraps her arms around her knees
squeezes her eyes shut
her body rocks back and forth

a tiny voice somewhere
far and deep
says,
what about what he did?
and what about what you did?

A thread

She can't not see him

she cleans
studies
keeps her voice soft
makes imperfect rotis
ties her hair back
takes care of her brother

but she can't not see Riv

they don't know
they don't know that without Riv
there is nothing to keep her here

he is the tiny
tiny thread
that keeps her
from floating away
and never coming back

How to man and woman

You have to be a man
Anji's mother used to say
to Surjit

how can you be a man
if you're always sick?
if you're not smart?
if you're failing in school?

Anji wants to ask her mother,
how do you fail second grade??

but her mother is not
asking that question

she is upset that
Surjit is not learning
how to man properly

that he's failing

and she's upset
that Anji is not
learning how to woman
properly
and that seems to be
no one's fault
but Anji's

her darker skin
too-wide nose
heavy voice
are all indicators
that Anji is failing too

but Anji's mother
is not mean about it

because she loves them
she is just trying
to help

the world is a harsh place,
she says,
and if you want to be happy
you have to be acceptable
respectable

she shows Anji
how to apply warm oil
to the sides of her nose
and squeeze the bridge
to make it thinner

she buys fairness creams
to help Anji's skin
become less dark
less unacceptable
because it will make life
easier,
she says

she finds tutors for Surjit
and urges him to do
things he's scared of
because real men
are not afraid

she works hard
to mold Anji and Surjit
into acceptable
respectable
versions of who they are

and it feels to Anji
like shoving your feet
into too-tight shoes

Anji watches her mother
do this every day to herself
worrying about what so-and-so said
and if people are going to think this or that

she wonders
if her mother realizes
this is the life she is shaping
for her children

are you happy, Mommy
Anji wants to ask

you are womaning
in all the right ways

your skin is light
your voice is soft and not too deep
your nose is straight and thin

you act smaller than you are
when men are around
you never let them see
the fierce intelligence
behind those eyes
doing all the right things
the accepted
respected things

are you happy?

Let's talk about love

Why Riv? Cathy asks
all this softness
in her voice
her hair is like a halo
around her head

the tears start
down Anji's face
at that softness

nobody's voice has any business
being that soft
that kind

but Anji thinks hard . . .

he's cute,
she says

but there are a lot of guys who are cute,
Cathy says,
why him?
what is it about him that has your heart racing?
is he a kind person...generous?
caring?
supportive . . . ?

for a moment Anji is blank
then she says slowly
I don't know . . . he feels familiar

ah, Cathy says
tell me more

something about the way he walks . . .
Anji closes her eyes to get the words

I can see him from all the way down the hall
at school – just a tiny glimpse
like the corner of his jacket even
and my heart starts pounding

Cathy nods
yes . . . your body knows, she says

but isn't that love?
Anji asks

let's talk about love for a minute,
Cathy says, sitting back
what does love look like for you?

Anji searches for words
it's just a feeling . . .

what feeling . . . tell me
describe it

I can't stop thinking about him
I want to be with him all the time
I can barely talk when I'm with him

and what do you know about him?
what do you love about him . . . ?

this question stumps Anji

Cathy's voice is gentle
when we love someone,
we love a lot of things about them
what makes them special, unique to us
we see them as they are
and love them
in all the different life scenarios
we witness them in

Anji is listening
no one has ever talked to her
about love before

it takes time to fall in love with someone, Anji
you have to get to know them

she leans forward
does this feel like the abuse
in any way?

Anji goes back
her body tightens
I don't understand, she says

what? Cathy asks
softly, very softly
what don't you understand?

the words come
from far back
so quiet and so thin

I don't understand, Anji says
he was a nice man
we laughed and played

I liked him, loved him maybe
he hugged me, held me
comforted me

when my mom and dad left
left me and Surjit there all day . . .
how was it abuse?

Cathy leans even further forward
her voice matching Anji's
whisper thin

he was an adult, she says gently
carefully, like with
a jittery bunny
and then her face hardens
he was an adult and you were a child

Cathy's words fall on Anji's skin
like raindrops
little tiny detonations

she wants more
then what do I feel for Riv? she asks

Cathy's eyes become tender
that's what we're going to figure out, honey

Chapter Five

Gradual

Anji Anji sat on a scorched wall
Anji Anji had a great fall
and all the people
in Anji's world
couldn't put Anji together again

in fact, no one knew she had fallen apart

now, she and Cathy are working together
to learn more about when and where
she fell and how to put her back together

Anji tells Cathy about things that happened
when she and her family still lived in India
and then what happened when they left

she tells Cathy
of how often she wants to turn to her mother
and say "please look at me
the way you look at Surjit"

sometimes she wanted to tear him
away from that place she has so longed to be
the special place reserved
only for him

inside the circle of her mother's arms
under the warmth of her gaze
was a spot with only his name on it

"you are my lucky child,"
her mother would say to Anji
and for a moment, that special smile
would light on Anji's face

"because after you
we were blessed with a boy"
a boy who made her mother
the mother of a son

Neesha Meminger

A big huge secret surprise

✦

I wish we celebrated Christmas,
Surjit says

I know, Anji says
let's pretend we do

she takes him to the window
look, she says, see all the stars?
that big bright one is Santa's sleigh

his eyes light up
is he coming here??

of course he is,
Anji says

will we get presents??

Anji knows there will be no presents
she knows they will go
to school after Christmas
and everyone will be talking
about what they got

and she and Surjit
and the other
non-Christian
immigrant kids like them
will have gotten nothing

and they will be outsiders again
in this country that is now their home

she knows that feeling
and she doesn't want him
to have it

maybe, she says,
maybe not

clouds pass over Surjit's eyes
and she quickly adds,
if we don't
it's only because
Santa has a bigger surprise for us later
a big huge secret surprise

excitement glows in his face again,
what kind of big huge secret surprise??

she shrugs,
who knows?
but it's going to be big
when we get it
and you can't tell anyone
or you might not get it

when they go back to school
after the holidays
she hears him telling his friends
that he didn't get anything
for Christmas

she feels a warmth in her belly
at the sound of
each of his words
filled to bursting
with joy
and hope

Wanting

There's always a "yummy" part
of abuse by a care giver,
Cathy says

that makes no sense,
Anji says,
the beginnings of a shout
rising in her body

big gold hoops dance
in Cathy's ears
as her hands explain

there's something in trauma
that we go back for
something that pulls us back
keeps calling until we go back
to get it

Anji shakes her head,
still don't get it

Cathy leans forward,
her nose ring glinting in the sun,
when the abuse is by a care giver
there is love entwined with the bad stuff
good feelings tangled up in there
with the horrible ones

Anji shifts in her seat,
she is uncomfortable inside
she doesn't like what's bubbling up,
are you saying I liked it?

Cathy shakes her head
vigorously
oh, goodness, not at all!
no, no, no

I mean that your body is a body
it responds as all animal bodies do
when we eat something good
smell something pretty
hear something beautiful . . .
we enjoy it

the body is programmed to enjoy
certain things . . .
hugs, kisses, warmth
intimacy, caresses, touch

it's perfectly normal
natural . . .
healthy,
she says emphatically

Anji nods slowly,
yes . . .
that's what was happening
hugs, fun, laughter, games

and it was happening,
Cathy says,
at the same time
as betrayal, fear, shattering
of trust

Anji doesn't nod
she is rearranging
things in her brain
making sense
out of what happened
with Cathy's new words

do you think you, Cathy says,
you might want to go back
and heal some of that?
we can go back together
so you're not alone this time

Anji stares at her
she has no words
everything inside
has vanished
but she wants more
more of the sense-making words

and somewhere
in the far far away deep
is a tiny wisp of a voice
that is getting stronger

it is laced with hope
like the light touch
of fingers
that smell of ghee

yes, it says
yes
I want to heal

When There Was Magic

There was a time,
Anji tells Cathy,
when I was happy

Cathy smiles
frosted purple lips say,
describe it to me

it was before we left India
there were all kinds of adults around
to take care of me
I trusted them and they were kind
loving

my parents were never alone
there was an entire village
to support them

I played in the fields
I loved being outside in the sun
I spread my arms and twirled
dancing and singing in the warmth
like a flower

and my grandmother
well, she wasn't actually my grandmother
she was my dad's step-aunt . . .
here, Anji's voice fades

Cathy prods gently
tell me about her

Anji's voice catches
but she breathes deep
and continues

she was blind
and she would trace my face
with her fingertips
her hands always smelled
like ghee and spices
and she would describe the strength in my nose
the beauty in my cheekbones
she would tell me my forehead
was like her great grandmother's

Anji's eyes sting
and tears drop
onto the backs of her hands
she reaches for a tissue

she loved me
she gasps,
she treasured me

Cathy nods,
it sounds like you were her entire world

there is silence for several minutes
and neither of them tries to fill it

then Cathy asks,
when was the last time you saw her?

Anji steadies her voice,
after we left India
she kept sending letters
and calling
begging my parents to bring me back
to let her see me one more time

but we never made it back
and she died a couple of years
after we left . . .

I never saw her again
and I never found that kind of love again
and my entire life shattered

Anji crumples into herself
sobbing with her entire body
for everything lost and stolen

Neesha Meminger

Healing

It's like a spiral staircase, Cathy says
you feel like you're at the same place sometimes
like you haven't gone anywhere
but you're higher up
you're always going up
you're never back to the same spot

keep going, she says
I'm right here
I'm not leaving

everyone leaves
Anji tell her
and sometimes they never come back

but there is always someone there
Cathy says with a smile
you'll see
just keep going
you can do it
I'm right here
I'm not leaving

Not Leaving

I'm not leaving,
Toni says
I'm staying my ass right here

do you think
they'll make you go?
Anji asks

Toni lights a cigarette
they'll try

where are they sending you?
Anji asks

Toni shrugs,
taking a deep drag

Anji doesn't want Toni to leave
going to and from school with Toni
is one of the best parts of Anji's day

when they walk
they get more time together
even if they don't talk much

and when they take the bus together
Toni says hilarious things
about the people they know from school

I hope you don't go,
Anji says quietly

Toni lifts one corner
of her mouth
into something that
could be a smile

What girls know

There are some things little girls
should never know,
Anji says

like what it's like
to lie
next to a naked grown man

Cathy nods quietly

Anji's voice is tight
stretched so thin
you almost don't know it's there

orgasms,
she says,
are for when you are
old enough
but when you are six
they split you in two

she is gripping the big rock
Cathy keeps on her table

she is breathing
like Cathy keeps reminding her to do

she is feeling the smoothness of the rock
the cool temperature of it
under her fingers

they make you
want to claw your way
out of your skin,
she says

they make you stand outside
your own self
and watch what's happening
to someone else
who looks like you

and you never really
ever
come back again
never really fit properly
back into that skin

because you aren't the same
and then there's a before
and an after

and you tear your body
from the inside out
sometimes from the outside in
and you pound it
you cut and you burn and you scream

you try to die

Anji's eyes sting
pool with tears she won't shed

these words that are coming
have never had room before
she will not shut them down now

because this place where you're supposed to live,
she says,
powering through

where you're supposed to exist
doesn't fit anymore

home doesn't recognize you
and you don't know
why it was you

why it happened to you

that's what orgasms do
to six-year-old girls,

she's sobbing now
there are some things,
she says faintly . . .
that little girls
should never ever
know

Chapter Six

Home

away from home.

her father's eyes are vacant
the man she once knew
is gone

her mother is the same
the same woman
the one who doesn't see her

when she turns to them,
her shelter in a storm,
they are the storm
cold blistering howling emptiness

there is no warmth
in their eyes
and there is no embrace
in their arms

home is a place she flees
even when she has
nowhere else to go

she flees whenever she can
she grasps for anything
that will keep her afloat
Riv
cigarettes
long island iced teas
spliffs
sex with Riv
or not with Riv

~ * ~

take care of your brother

and she did
she took care of him
as best she could
as completely as any child could

and then
when she looked around

she was alone

~ * ~

they were already broken
before moving to the new country
they brought their brokenness
in their bones
across the stretch of black sea

they settled
running from old wounds
hoping
hoping for new winds
to bring new balms

but the old wounds
seeped into the bones
of their children
brought over from a long line
of wounding

this new land
that did not welcome them
was not what broke them

the breaking came earlier
more ancient
more primal

a rape that happened
within our own circles
our own families
the places we felt safe
the sacred places

that's where the first wounding was,
on hallowed ground
the most holy of sites

separating
body
home
it separated
tearing everything apart

a long wail flung
across generations
repeating, echoing
until someone said
enough

and that someone
was me

Neesha Meminger

Fires

❖

There are fires that destroy
fires that warm
fires that cook
or light a path

the fire that Anji watched
blazing in the windows of her
first home in the new country

had been set by the boys
her father had gone downstairs
to confront
with other men who stood
with him to "stare down
fear and hate"

but fear and hate,
Anji realized,
were an out-of-control fire
that swallowed homes
and dreams
and sometimes people

the boys had painted words
on the sides of the building
words that shouted
words that taught fear
words that destroyed

at school Anji's teachers
told her that words
can't hurt
sticks and stones can

Anji watched the hate
scrawled across the bricks
of her family's home
char and blacken with smoke

she smelled wood burning
wood that had been cool under bare feet
she heard the roar of and swoosh of fire
sweeping through rooms she'd napped in
played with her dolls in

she looked at her mother
standing shoulder to shoulder
with her father
both of them staring up
at the flames leaping into the night sky

she held tight to Surjit's shoulders
as people ran and shouted around her

her father had grabbed her
holding her askance and stumbling down stairs
her mother was behind, holding a groggy Surjit

hate is not dark,
Anji thought,
hate is . . . blazing and white hot
lighting up the midnight sky
loud and bold and unashamed

hate, when confronted
slinks away
but it comes back in the night
when you're not looking
when you're sleeping

it tries to swallow you whole

and if you're not careful
it will take everything you have
the floor you walk on
the shelter above your head

Anji was learning
to be careful
to know danger
before it arrived

to step gingerly, deftly
before she was struck
to shed her skin and grow a new one
depending on where she was
who she was with

to learn the language of
bank school home
unemployment office
laundromat
police station
fire department

and the old country
where someone was there
to make cricket bats for her
or lovingly trace the features of her face

that country was a wisp
of disappearing smoke
this was a world
where you had to step carefully

Neesha Meminger

there were no bombs or explosions
but there was danger
in the darkness
waiting for you to come to it
and then swallowed you whole
if you weren't careful

Holy men

Tell me about
the temple,
Cathy asks

that makes it different,
she says

what we're taught
about religion
about men who preach
the word of god…
it has a whole different
impact when there is abuse
within that context

Anji thinks hard
about this thing
she has never thought about before

holy men,
she says,
are just men

they run a holy house
a templechurchmosquesynagogue
a sanctuary
but do they become gods?

my mom thought so

because we were in a holy building
my mom thought we'd be safe
she never, in her wildest dreams
or nightmares
could have imagined what
we were going through

but I know,
Anji says,
peeling back the years

holy men
are just men

they don't transcend
suddenly superhuman
suddenly holy

through studies
degrees vows promises

to my mother
they were holy
not capable of committing
abominations

men of faith
with a direct line
to the divine

absolute power
over small bodies
unquestioned

the complete faith
of worshippers
desperate

be a good child
don't make trouble

it fucks with your trust,
Anji says,

Cathy nods,
and with your faith

Anji's chin trembles
yes, she whispers
when I'm at my lowest
how do I hope?

if god could allow these things
on holy ground
where do I go
when there's nowhere to go?

Trickery

There's something else,
Cathy says

there's this thing
that happens for survivors,
around being tricked

with children
abusers are careful
they have to draw a child in
with things like candy
puppies kittens
maybe the possibility of love

hugs, Anji says
cuddles
warmth
things that aren't at home

yes, Cathy says
her words an embrace,
and so survivors are very sensitive
to trickery
she pauses for a moment

that must have been amplified
for you
in what your parents
the people you trusted most in the world
considered a house of god
the ultimate power in the universe

she watches Anji's face
for a moment
before continuing

we learn about god,
she says,
at home
when we learn about trust

when we trust caretakers
we learn about having faith

Anji is trying hard to follow
Cathy's words
but it's a dance
where she flits
out of her body
every now and then
and she has to bring herself back

faith is what trust becomes
when it grows up,
Anji says,
digesting
trying to grasp the words
and keep them in her hands
so they can become part of her body

when our caretakers cannot be trusted,
Cathy says,
then we can easily be tricked
into handing our faith,
that most powerful hope-giver, life-sustainer
over to kind-faced liars

at this, Anji looks up
into Cathy's face
and knows
that Cathy understands

Chapter Seven

On holy ground

Anji is turning things over
in her head
looking at them carefully

Rihanna has a song
with the word *erotic* in it
Anji looks up *eros*

it's a feeling
in the body –
the skin muscles
flesh senses

but it's a feeling
inside the body, too –
the heart mind
feelings imagination

and she looks up
the word faith

and sees how they are
the same
to her

she starts writing
what her body is trying to shape
into words
Rihanna's melody floating on pain
seeping into long-forgotten crevices

she tries to wrap words
around the tender, screaming
holes in her body

sex and spirit
sexuality defiled
spirituality snuffed

both flickering flames
in the wind
one puff

and you can blow
either of them out
amputating a whole chunk of a person

eros erotic erogenous
Anji turns the words over
in her mouth

it should belong to her
this thing that has to do with
body with desire

desire is wanting
a push an urge a spark
the beginning

it makes you move
it stirs
starts the process of living

of life
of creating
of everything

trust is
faith is
spirit

it's the thing
that is not the body
the thing inside

when Anji closes
her eyes
the thing inside is spirit

the thing inside
that still sings
that still can see light

even when her eyes
are closed
that is spirit

it should be hers
this thing
that can see light in the dark

but when trust
is broken
faith cracks and crumbles

and spirit wavers
that faint, serpentine curl
of smoke

that sustains life
that brings hope
that shows light when it's dark

it does only what
it was programmed
to do

the animal of me,
Anji thinks softly
it just does what it was meant to do

eyes closed
both rising and undulating
in the dark

like flowers reaching
for the sun
both celebrating

life
being alive
grateful and joyful

two sides
of the same coin,
Anji thinks

and then wonders,
what happens
to the heart

when these two
mighty threads
are separated?

Peonies

Tearing away from Riv
feels like peeling off her own skin

Cathy is there
like the sun
and Anji turns to her
follows her warmth
when she feels like she is dying

Cathy catches her, always
just like she promised

sometimes, Anji wants to share
what she is learning
with her mother

some of the things she is understanding
about the past
about their family
about children and parents
and faith and trust
and healing

her mother doesn't like any of it
she doesn't trust the counselors
she doesn't trust this foreign woman
that Anji makes appointments
twice a week to see

they are going to turn you against us,
she says,
they will destroy our home
and our family
they don't understand our ways
our culture
our traditions

and Anji holds her words
like pebbles in her mouth

our culture
our traditions
have shattered me
into slivers of a whole
I will never become again

I am bleeding, mommy
on my hands and knees
in all of that brokenness
trying to find myself

but she says nothing
turns away
and swallows the hard stones
in her mouth

A group of one's own

Cathy wants Anji to join a group
it's a group of girls
survivors, she calls them

they all went through something
like what Anji did
and they're all around her age

you might even know some of them,
she says

Cathy peers at her
through thick purple glasses
think about it, she says
it might help you to feel less alone

but nothing really bad happened to me, Anji says

Cathy nods

those girls probably went through really horrible
bad stuff

Cathy nods again

no one hurt me, Anji says
no one really actually hurt me
like, I wasn't violently raped or anything
some girls are

Cathy's words are soft,
and yet here you are
with me

Anji stares out the window
but that's because of the sadness
I can't get away from the sadness

Cathy's eyes rest gently on Anji's face
these girls, she says
they are dealing with some of the same things
at home, at school, with boyfriends and girlfriends
with their bodies and inside their bodies

we work through things with art
sometimes, when people are hurt
before they have words for what
is happening to them
it's hard for them to talk or put
words to their feelings

Anji sits still
something deep inside her
is listening very carefully

so it can be easier,
Cathy says,
to make something that shows the feeling
or to speak through art

would you like to try that?

Anji has no words
her body is quiet
listening

think about it, Cathy says again,
very gently

Others

The group is five girls

Toni is there
something lights up inside Anji
yet she is not entirely surprised to see her

Toni smiles
a real smile this time
and doesn't seem surprised to see Anji, either

but aside from exchanging smiles
neither of them says anything

on the bus Toni is always pulling her sleeves down
but here she doesn't hide the marks
there are cuts and burns and some bruises
Anji wonders if Toni did them all herself

they go around and "check in"
just saying how they are feeling
right now in the moment

Cathy is gentle but she prods carefully
like nudging a sleeping giant
like she wants to get something out
without waking a beast

Anji listens mostly
during check in she says she's nervous
and doesn't know if she really belongs here

Toni stares at her, then says
you belong here

Cathy quickly but gently says
no interruptions, please
was there anything else you wanted to share, Anji?

Anji shakes her head

when it's Toni's turn, she looks at Anji
you belong here, she says again
we all think everyone else has gone through worse
that we're just complaining for no reason

that's what abusers want us to think
whether they're your father
or a fascist dictator
they want us to believe
that what we have to say
is not important

but it is
and we're here
and it was horrible
and it shouldn't have happened
and
      it's
           not
                your
                      fault

another girl, Sara, says she's nervous
about her upcoming court case
her stepfather will be there
with her brother
and they might make her go back
to live with him
because her mother doesn't have a job

that's gonna suck,
another girl, Gina, says

Anji has never ever been in a room
where people talk like this
where you can say your father raped you
or your grandfather molested you
and no one is freaked out
or yelled at

they just listen and nod
and sometimes they agree
and sometimes they say that fucking sucks

and sometimes they say
it was not your fault

Chapter Eight

Flight

She knows she has to leave
this home is becoming
like the dark jaws in her dreams
no solace
no haven

but how?

it is home
it is family
it is all she knows

what will she find
out there?

I don't know
but I can't stay here

here are dreams wilted
turned to sludge
beneath trudging feet
bitter cold aloneness
stolen joy

every day Anji wakes up
hoping to have a good day
and every night lies down
hollow, depleted

her voice
ricocheting
in what feels like
a cavernous and echoey
expanse

she wants to turn to her mother
but she sees the lines
of an ancient sorrow
etched into her face
layers of pain in her eyes

her mother's body
shows lines of remembering
a family disappointed with
the first girl-child

mothers sending sons to school
and keeping daughters home
fathers drinking their bodies
into the ground
gambling away the children's future

Anji's father is here and not here
cushioned away from
anything that reminds him
of memories that could destroy him

a Punjab being strangled
by its own government
farmers desperate
and committing suicide
their children taking off
to cities or drowning
in their own addictions

there was no future there,
her father whispers

this was what was behind
what they'd left
so the children
could find hope

they cannot see Anji's pain
because it might show them their own
and that would undo everything

Surjit needs her
but she can't help him
because she doesn't know
how to help herself

she's slipping

Anji writes and writes
and writes
and feels so utterly
alone

she knows
she has to leave
this home has become
like the dark jaws
in her dreams

Belonging

The group is every Tuesday after school
for an hour and a half
there are five girls
Anji, Toni, Sara, Gina, and Rose

Anji looks forward to it
counts the hours
every single week

they are all broken
misshapen
half-gone
bleeding
hurt

but mending

sometimes Anji talks
sometimes she says nothing
and listens
pays attention, like Cathy said

she drops into her body
is anything tensing up?
does her heart start racing?
does she space out?

listening is sometimes better than talking
because even though
they all went through different things
like really different
they all say almost the same things

like they can't feel things
like they see other people and feel
like they're in a different world
like no one ever sees them
like they're screaming and screaming
and screaming, but no one hears

sometimes Cathy throws a pillow in the middle
and says, that's him
what do you want to say to him?

one time Toni jumped on the pillow
and tore it apart
tiny white feathers flying everywhere
they were floating around them
all through the session
her face was red and she was screaming
you had no right

Anji doesn't know what happened to Toni
but she doesn't have to
she knows how Toni feels
and what she's fighting when she's on that pillow
Anji has never wanted to tear a pillow apart before
but seeing Toni do it makes it just seem right

sometimes Cathy puts an empty chair
in front of one of the girls
and says say it directly to her
tell your mother
what you wish she had done

she did this to Anji once
and words evaporated
her body was short circuiting everywhere

that was when Gina said, real quiet,
it's okay
you're safe
no one will hurt you here

and Anji felt something come loose
a tiny something shifting...taking root
but no words

Rose said something Cathy asked a lot,
how old do you feel, Anji?
that's when Anji realized
there were no words
because she was too little inside
to know what some things were called

A larger plan

They sometimes get bubble tea after group
not everyone can stay after
but Anji and Toni almost always go
sometimes Sara comes too
but Gina and Rose almost never do

it's a way to get back into the world again, slowly
a reminder that the world
doesn't have the same rules as group
but that group lingers with you even after you go out
into the 'real world'

I would never have known
all this about you, Toni says
she's having mango bubble tea

Anji sips on her taro one

I thought you were just like
all the other Indian girls
following the rules
quiet
smart

Anji smiles
I am, she says

Toni laughs
I mean, she says
for a long time
I didn't think this kinda thing happened
in your homes like it happened in mine
I thought it was just a Puerto Rican thing
. . . maybe a Latina thing

Rose is Vietnamese,
Anji points out

yeah, and Gina's Italian
my father's Iranian,
Sara says,
and my mother's Guyanese

Toni spins her cup
it just sucks,
she says

girls are raped
even if every inch of their bodies
is covered,
Sara says,
from head to toe

Anji looks at Toni
I wasn't raped

no, Toni says
but what happened to you
shouldn't have happened
you were too small
and those men knew
what they were doing
children can't consent

Sara touches Anji's shoulder
you trusted them to keep you safe
your parents trusted them to keep you safe
they took advantage of all that trust

Anji's skin feels tight
I ran to him
I needed him to hold me
I wanted someone to hold me
so bad

tears sting her eyes
pool in the corners
and spill
her voice comes out
thin and flimsy

I liked him, she says

Toni clenches her jaw
of course you did
he was nice to you
and you were a kid
kids can be lured with candy
and cuddly animals
grown men know that

her voice is not thin at all
they took away your choice,
she says,
you didn't get to choose
when you wanted to be touched
and by who

they took advantage,
Sara says,
of your trust
and vulnerability
all kids need hugs
all kids need to feel safe

Anji swallows hard,
struggling to pull herself together
she turns to Toni,
I saw you on the bus all the time,
and in the halls at school and had no idea

Toni holds up her arms with the scars
really? she smiles
I was kinda advertising it

Anji shrugs
yeah, really
I had no idea

we're all good at putting on
a public face,
Sara says,
we think it protects us
protects our families
we try to be good
so maybe love will find us
maybe love will save us

Toni takes a deep breath and exhales
I was never good
my sister was good and she was getting
shit on just as much as I was

she looks at Anji
I don't like talking to people at school
I don't care what they think
I know what they say about me
but most of them aren't worth talking to

Anji smiles
I am
but you wouldn't have known it
if I didn't come to group

Sara grins
I am, too
and if we were all in the same school
we would be a legendary squad

Toni gives a short chuckle
if neither of you came to group
I wouldn't be talking to you
I totally believe there's a larger plan
and we meet the people we're meant to meet

true, Sara says
and they're all quiet again

Gina

My father acted like
I was his girlfriend
when I was three
he said mom was jealous of our relationship
and we were going to live together

happily ever after
I was a princess
and he my prince
he was saving me

he waited to touch me
until I was old enough
and then he said you're ready now

he didn't hurt me
his fingers
like a cold fish
slippery and slimy

I floated away
threw up

it was our secret
mine and daddy's
I kept it like a good girl

I felt special
I was a princess
how many other girls are actual princesses he'd say
happily ever after

I held it for him
his secret

Getting stronger

He's standing before her
beautiful perfect
let's forget everything, he says
let's start over
me and you
let's go somewhere together and never come back

she closes her eyes
turns her face up
there is no sun
just a mist coming down
from where the sun should be

Riv . . .

she's gotten so used to repeating
his name
like prayer beads around her neck
drops of blood pulsing through her veins

there is a part of her
a long ago far away very young part
that ran desperately after her father

and watched a giant heavy door
slam behind him
trapping her in a place that would
destroy parts of her

she wants to run through that door
before it closes again
before he is lost again to her
forever

and most of her squeezes through
but this time
there are more parts of her
other parts that have been growing up
getting stronger

I want to heal, they say

Sara

The door was open
he was eighteen
she was twelve
their parents left him in charge
he was watching something online
his hand down his pants
she walked in

the door was open she sobbed
he was supposed to be looking out for me
I was hungry the door was open
c'mere, he said, I want you to do this thing for me
if you tell
I'll kill you I swear to god

and I did it she says
words all splintered
I did it
but it didn't stop
I thought it would stop
they tumble out
awkward
snagging on sharp edges
in her throat

Chapter Nine

Love is a language

Will I ever meet someone
who can love me?

Cathy's eyes
flutter to Anji's face
like a down feather
of course, she says
you have so much to offer

then why hasn't anyone seen that?
if I'm wonderful and lovable
why didn't anyone ever see that?
pins prick the backs of her eyes
they fill, threatening to spill over

for a minute
the question hangs there

Cathy shifts in her seat
she's looking at the table
like she's sifting through words
for the right ones

you can't control what people see, she says
you can't control what they value
people can only value others
as much as they value themselves

but why me?
there are families out there who value
their kids . . .

do you think your parents
never loved you, Anji?

Anji pauses
no...I think they did love me
I think they still do . . .
maybe in the only way they know how

she looks at Cathy
but it doesn't feel like love
to me

you speak different languages,
Cathy says gently
love is a language
and the one your parents speak
is different from the one you've
learned to speak

Anji's heart twists
but why?

Cathy tilts her head to one side
it's hard to know, she says,
exactly what messages
we absorb and where they all come from

so how am I supposed to find it, then?
love, I mean
if my own mother and father
could leave me in the arms
of men
strangers . . .
she doesn't know how to finish

something flits across Cathy's face
they thought, hon,
that they were doing the right thing

they probably thought
like a lot of people
that the church
or in your case, the temple
was the safest place they could leave you

in their minds
and their hearts
they thought they were leaving
their children
their most precious loves
in a sacred and holy place
well protected and cared for

that is what a church
or any other holy place
is supposed to be,
right?

well,
Anji whispers fiercely
it wasn't

Cathy inches forward
in her chair
you,
she whispers, just as fiercely
you will see
just how important you are

but then will I be alone
for the rest of my life?

Cathy shakes her head
when you find love
deep inside
and realize
you *are* love
you will never again
be alone

Anji doesn't know what that means
but she sits with the words
Cathy's words
in her chest
very very close to her heart

she will hold them to the light
afterward
at home
when she's alone in her bedroom
and look at them from different angles

and write them down
and write others down
to try to make sense out of it all

but I want hugs,
she says to the empty room
and someone to tell me they love me
and I want kisses
like the sun

she remembers that look
that sometimes comes over Cathy's face
remembers Cathy saying
in words that are tender
angel wings
wrapping around hurt places

I pray that you will
have lots of love, Anji
that you have
so many people
always

I believe
she squeezes her eyes closed
that they will find you

Anji stares at the backs of her hands
and remembers another pair of deep brown hands
older, wizened, aged with love

she remembers the warmth of other words
from the distant past
somewhere far and distant
and deep down,
echoed in Cathy's blessing

slowly the tears subside
and she is able to sleep

Inheritance

Anji remembers the old woman
the blind woman they said was her great aunt
she remembers her in wisps and shadows
she remembers the feel of fingertips
and the smells
of diesel and ghee and guavas

the woman had told her stories
about snake whisperers
and women and magic and power

"no one speaks openly about them,"
she'd say
"but women like that have always existed, child"

the woman's brother, Anji's great uncle
would scoff
"nonsense," he'd boom
"stupid, superstitious nonsense
stop feeding the child your silly woman's beliefs"

but the women of the village
had been passing down stories
through generations,
she'd say,
they would whisper their truths
and sacred stories

they would gather at night
under the pippal tree
hundreds of years old
they said
they'd gather under the full moon
on the hill past the fields

they would gather and
tell the forbidden stories
about snake whisperers

"the snake charmers you see in the cities
and traveling through the villages to make
a few paisas, they are all men now," she'd whisper
"they make a mockery of the truth"
she would spit the words out in disdain
"no one charms a snake
serpents do not dance to a flute"

"you are one of them,"
the old woman would tell her
"like me
and many, many before
we go so far back . . .
maybe to the original"

"wherever you go, my angel,"
she said,
"the serpent spirit will find you"

some of the woman's stories
stayed with Anji
over continents and a vast stretch
of black water

over years that would take her
far, far away from herself
only to bring her right back to the beginning . . .

"right before I lost my eyesight
I saw one of the largest king cobras
I'd ever seen
he was behind the chullah
when I was making rotis

"I didn't see him at first
because he blended so completely
with the colors of the earthen oven
and the shadows of the evening

"when I reached to flip a roti
my arm was snatched from behind
by my brother

"he dragged me from the stool
I'd been sitting on
he could have woken the ancestors
he was shouting so loudly
and making no sense whatsoever

"several men from the surrounding homes

"heard and came running"

Anji remembers that the old woman's voice
became tormented then,
as she recalled the details after that

"I shouted and screamed for them to stop
but they would not listen . . .
that poor sacred creature
lying lifeless . . .
oh, how could they do such a thing!"

one time she told Anji
about a lovely copper cobra
that slithered up one of the fat legs
of a manja in the courtyard

"I'd laid you down," she said,
"when you were an infant"
here, Anji remembered
the woman paused to lay a warm
ghee-scented hand on Anji's arm

"the serpent curled up for a nap at your feet
it was a good omen
a blessing"
she'd smooth Anji's hair
and gently trace the girl's features again
feeling for the expression on the child's face

"I watched the two of you sleep
for some time
then I thanked the holy mother
for the blessing
before quietly and carefully
retrieving you"

"I knew, then
that you were mine"
she'd said
"no matter whose gate
you entered through . . .
you belonged to me"

she then quietly sent word to the village women
about the serpent in her courtyard

she knew the men would kill
that shimmering beauty
but the women had other methods,
she'd say,
with just a hint of a smile on her lips

and then she'd snap her eyes open
and, just as suddenly as she'd started,
she would come to an abrupt stop

~ * ~

Anji had had a visit
the night before
the old woman had died

a giant copper colored cobra
hood fanned out
entire length illuminated
as if from within
swaying at the foot of her bed
as Surjit slept soundly
in his bed next to her

she hadn't been afraid
she'd stared at it
and felt only a warm
loving light

when Anji told her mother
of the serpent that had visited
during the night
"sheer nonsense"
her mother had said
Anji knew her mother
hated serpents of all kinds

"there are no cobras in this country
they can't live in the cold
you were dreaming"

but Anji knew what she'd seen
and she knew it had not been a dream
she'd been wide awake
and no part of it felt like nonsense

it had been the realest thing she'd
experienced
since they'd arrived
in the new country

Toni

I was in the bathroom
my dad no not my stepdad
my dad
walked in on me
he didn't live with us
I didn't even know he was my father
I'd grown up with a different man
Miguel
thinking he was my father
but Shaun, my dad
came back
and my mom wanted me to know
my dad

she and Miguel had split up a year before
maybe she called Shaun then
maybe she couldn't be alone without a man
for a single minute
I don't know

but I was in the bathroom
and this man
my dad
walked in
threw me to the ground
punched me in the face
pinned my arms down
and tore me open
felt like I split
from the top of my head
down
that was my dad
14

my mom threw him out
as soon as I told her
but we never talked about it again
and she made me go and visit him

he's still your father she said

yes . . .
he's still my dad

Chapter Ten

Courts

So many of the girls
have court dates

Anji already had hers
with Riv
she could still remember
his sister's whispers
whore!

and yet
Anji's was not as bad
as some of the other girls'

her father or brother
or grandfather
or mother
were not there
her parents didn't even know

Anji had gone through hers
alone

they were not the ones
on the other side

it has to happen on all the levels
Gina says
they get you in your house
they get you in the culture
and in tradition
and then they get you in the courts

if they don't get us on all the levels
they can't keep all of us down
they have to make sure we can't get up
that there's no way for us to get up

because if even one of us gets up
others will think they can, too

like slaves, Toni says
they couldn't gather in groups
they couldn't sing their songs
or dance their dances

Gina nods,
and Indigenous peoples
songs and dances were illegal
like, you could go to jail
if you danced

because it was threatening,
Sara says, joins in
when we sing our songs
and dance our dances
we connect with the divine
we are empowered
we communicate directly with god

we don't need a middle man
says Toni

they can't control us
Gina continues
the only way to control us
is on all the levels

Neesha Meminger

Splitting

Tell me about the sadness,
Cathy says

Anji can barely get out the words
it's not fair

Cathy nods
what's not fair

I didn't get what I was supposed to get
when I was little
and now I have to be grown
and not expect anyone to take care of me
but when I was supposed to expect it
when I *needed* it
no one did

no, it's not fair at all

and all that love
and attention I'm desperate for

how old is that part of you
Cathy says
the desperate one

Anji shrugs
maybe four?

Cathy's face looks tender
hmm, she says
just a baby

what does she need?
she asks
are there any words
any shapes or colors
images
that come to mind

Anji's brain tries
to make sense of this
but it scrambles
and fizzles

she tries to grab the words
scans her brain for images
she studies them
like a math problem

when we are hurt,
Cathy says, trying again
the wound gets stuck there
and we move around it
like a big hole in the road

you know when you have a physical
wound?
like when you took a nasty
spill on your bike when you were a kid . . .
skinned knees, cuts, bruises, blood . . . ?

Anji nods

well, when a child falls
and gets a booboo
she tells everyone she sees about it
look mommy, I got a booboo
look aunt so-and-so, I got a booboo
look grandma, I got a booboo
and everyone clucks and coos
and kisses the booboo better
and soothes the child

Anji nods. she has seen this
with Surjit and cousins
and children on the subway
in the park

and then after a while
the booboo begins to heal,
Cathy says softly

first there is a bandage to protect it
while the body begins the healing process
and then after a certain point
when there is a scab
when the blood has crusted over
the tender skin
the bandage comes off
so the sun and air can help

the scab can fall off then
because underneath is a
shiny new
much tougher skin

Cathy pauses for a moment
to read Anji's face
then continues

inside booboos
or emotional wounds
from trauma are the same
except we don't get to
tell

hey mommy, I got a booboo
hey aunt so-and-so, I got a booboo
hey grandma, I got a booboo

Anji shakes her head
no we don't tell she says
sometimes telling can get us
in deep trouble
or thrown out of the house

yes, Cathy says
we are expected to go on
keep silent
sometimes even protect those
who did the hurtful things

Anji studies Cathy's words
concentrating
examining them carefully in her head
when you speak up, she says,
people get mad
they want you to keep quiet

Cathy nods
because sometimes the way things are
and your silence
works better for the people
around us
in our families, in the world

it allows them to stay
in control
allows them to keep
having their own needs met
to keep the focus on themselves

Anji nods,
and meanwhile we are left behind
. . . being good students
good girls
obedient because
we think it will bring us
love

Cathy holds her gaze,
yes, that it will turn the favor
of the adults around us
toward us
and that's what we're all looking for
isn't it
love?

Anji nods again
she knows that ache
that hollowness
well

Cathy continues
so we keep living life like
nothing happened
like there's no booboo

except there is
Anji says
you can't pretend it away

Cathy nods again,
you can't pretend it away,
she repeats softly
and because we can't tell
and because we can't acknowledge it
the body doesn't know
how to heal it

but it wants to

yes
so it keeps sending you
these signals

pain is the body's way of
communicating with you
it's like a child tugging at
her mommy's skirt

and, like the annoyed mommy
who has so many things to do
who has a hectic life to tend to,
we swat the pain away

but it doesn't go away

Cathy shakes her head
it keeps waiting there
until we look at it again
until we cluck and coo at it
and give it exactly what it needed
when it happened

Anji sits back, understanding
because it never grew up!

Cathy smiles,
it never grew up

but I grew around it

yes
and here you are,
but the booboo
it's still all the way back there
exactly the same as the moment
it happened

that's why it feels so deep
so fresh

yes
because it's way down
inside
back where there's a six-year-old
still waiting to show everyone
her booboo
still waiting to be seen

and this is how it hurt
then
to her
         to me
her . . . me
she is me and I'm her
but the booboo
it's hers from then

and yours, Cathy says
it's both
together
what we're doing
is separating the then and there
from the here and now,
she says,
peering intently at Anji

you have grown
around the booboo
but it's stuck there
ignored, unseen
even by you

everyone left her
back there
she's still waiting

Cathy nods, and adds
but she's safe now
no one will ever hurt
that six-year-old like that again
because she has you

Cathy's face
is a silent reflection
of Anji's pain
cloaked tenderly
in something so caring
that Anji can't look at her
for very long

I have to go back
and get her,
she says,
her voice wobbling

she's still there
waiting
that's why it hurts
so much
everyone left her

Anji whispers something else
but no words come out

they are still there
held tight
in the past...
in the tightened chest
of a six-year-old

Chapter Eleven

Neesha Meminger

Learning

❖

The men were good men, holy men,
her parents said
they trusted them

be a good girl
don't make trouble
Daddy will pick you up tonight

one man was funny
young, like an uncle she'd left in the old country
he played fun games, cuddled her, and laughed

he gave lots of hugs

he taught her how to play the tabla
and the punjabi letters
rhythms of the old country

her parents were pleased

Anji liked the young man
the fun one who reminded her of an uncle
he played the games in the small
room behind the closed doors
he made her laugh
tickled her

she didn't have to fly away . . . not right away

180

until the laughing stopped
and everything shifted
just a small whisper

she didn't always fly away
sometimes she went deep inside
deep, deep, far down
under thick, heavy layers
until she couldn't hear anything
feel anything
remember anything

except the old woman
smiling, weathered
whispering things about magic
and power

"wounds weep"
the old woman had said
urgently, desperately
"do you understand, child?
old, deep wounds, they wail
until you hear them
until you come for them

"they yank you from wherever you are
and bring you tearing back
to the moment they were created"

"pay attention, my love"
the creased face said
"to that dark place
that made you run"

Rose

My uncle and my grandfather
on my mother's side
we all lived together in one house
on one floor

we were saving money
keeping our eye on the dream
running a business
working hard

I played piano
impeccably
I was impeccable
three sisters
we were all going through it

but none of us talked about it
when everyone went to sleep
my grandfather came into our bedroom
pretending he was soothing us to sleep
everyone acted like they were asleep

I acted like I was asleep
I was wooden
frozen

her face is stiff when she says this
but in her eyes
there are storms raging
destructive
furious
hurricanes

I set the house on fire
they ruled it an accident
but I did it
quietly
calmly

I saw how on youtube
you can learn how to do anything
on youtube
. . . and if there was no house
everyone couldn't live in it

we would move
or rebuild
maybe I would have a room
to myself
where I could lock
the door

fire burns wood
it unfreezes

fire rages
it is not stiff
silent
frozen

it rages

Neesha Meminger

And then there were four

❖

They lost Gina
she missed group
once
twice
three times

and then Cathy told them
Gina's not coming back
let's talk about this

you would think
they'd have questions
you would think
they'd wonder why

but they knew

they hurt
each of them in their own ways
Gina was fierce
and now it was like
they were cracked
not whole
another wound

Gina had a court case

in the last group session
she cried
that kind of whole body crying
when everything inside you
is screaming

they're going to make me
go back there
she'd said

Gina was a minor
her mother wasn't working
she was an alcoholic with an arrest record
her older sister, Rosalia, wanted custody
but she wasn't 18 yet

there was no one else
and her father wanted her back
had a lot of money
and was fighting to get her back
she has a brother, he said
a brother who looks out for her

her father was a good man, they said
respected, well to do
able to give her a good future
put her through college
well regarded in the community
very very successful

the girls knew

how judges
who were mostly men
saw things
how cops
who were mostly men
saw things
how this world
run mostly by men
saw things

they knew
they'd all seen

Toni stood up
flipped her chair
shouted cursed
stormed

Anji imploded
without a word

Rose cried
and Sara made soft, soothing sounds
maybe to herself
maybe to Rose
maybe to all of them,
Anji didn't know

A core glowing ember

Let's write a group poem,
Cathy says
look at the artwork you just created
and see what it speaks to you
just listen quietly
to what it's saying
and then write
whatever comes up

each girl is
in her own world
with the colors and shapes
that have come out of her

each girl has plucked things
from somewhere inside or outside of her
and breathed life into them
giving them form
on a piece of paper
or fabric

Anji looks at hers
a swirl of colors
lots of energy and flow
but no concrete shape

and still, there are feelings there
she feels them as she looks at
what has come out of her

words form in her consciousness
not in her mind or in her heart
but somewhere close
somewhere just outside of her
and she plucks them out
once they are clear

when the girls meet again
in the center
they share their words
and a poem comes together . . .

everything we are
every moment
we live
we breathe
it's all still there

it doesn't just go away
because you've slipped
into a new moment

it's all still there inside
breathing
living

it's there every day
when you
make decisions
pick lovers
find friends
choose jobs

it's always there
each moment of bliss
of elation
relief

and that moment
the first time
you were hit
screamed at
told to go back
where you come from

or when
grown up fingers pried
open parts of your
young tender body

they're all there
pixels that make up
a whole

you build around them
they never go away

they are what makes
up your skin
blood cells flowing
through your veins

that little girl
in the center of your body
right there
maybe above your bellybutton
below your chest
in your muscles
in your bones
there, still

waiting . . .

I love our poem,
Sara says softly

me, too,
Rose says

it feels unfinished,
Anji says

Cathy smiles,
and that's okay, too
she says,
it's *becoming*

Chapter Twelve

Memory

I haven't seen Riv
in three months,
Anji says

Cathy nods
I know, she says
she flips through her notes
and tells Anji the exact date
they last talked about him

and what's going on
inside,
Cathy asks, leaning closer

Anji's voice is tight
it's hard,
she says
I miss him

him?
Cathy asks,
or something else?

Anji ponders this

when he kissed me
I flew

something in me lifted
my body rose
opened
I felt alive
in ways I normally don't

Anji looks into Cathy's face
there is understanding there
no judgment
no scorn

she continues,
inside I felt a voice saying,
he's come back

he's come back!
he's come back!

who's come back,
Cathy asks

Anji shakes her head
I don't know

but for that moment
every moment we touched
we kissed
we made out
or had sex

her eyes flick back to Cathy's face
before continuing

I sort of . . .
felt like I was with god
like . . . whole
loved
complete

for just that moment
and then I would come down
crashing back to reality
full of debris and
discarded things

and I would feel like
I'd lost everything
the entire world

after having met him
fallen for him
actually, I didn't fall for him
I kind of plunged off a cliff
into him . . .
I feel like my heart
beats differently now

good different?
Cathy asks

Anji thinks about that
for a moment

yes, she says
Riv was a crappy boyfriend
but being with him
showed me
parts of myself

Cathy raises an eyebrow
tell me more

he showed me what was hurt,
Anji says

Cathy gives the slightest nod,
her eyes shimmering
unshed tears

Play

In the temple
the men played games
with the children
in the small room
behind the big closed doors

Anji didn't know
how many children or when
and if they all played the same games
around nap time
when they were alone in the
small room with the mattress
on the floor

but this is when Anji learned to fly
while sitting in one place

she could see what was happening
in other parts of the temple
the old woman stirring pots in the
giant kitchen downstairs
making food for the hungry
because that is what good people
do when they believe in god
when they have faith

she could see the other children playing downstairs
like children are supposed to
because it was her nap time right now
theirs would come, maybe later
or maybe it already had

she saw them playing
it was where she should have been
kicking a ball with other children
like children do

and she flew up
over her body and his
out
away
free

Create

My dreams have been
super crazy lately,
Anji says in group

last night
there was fire on the water

I've been having a lot
of fire dreams too,
Rose says
tell me about yours

we were all there
all of us, even Gina

and there was this energy
that moved up
from the base of our bodies
through the center

curling around our spines
like serpents going up a staff

the energy rose like fire
into the night
sparks rising to the heavens
flames reaching like arms

swaying serpents mesmerized
by a call that we all understood
but no one around us did

we were dancing
and it was night

there was a beat attacking our ears
like explosions
incessant
urging us to rise

and somewhere there was a voice
it was saying,
all the saviors have left
the doors have slammed

fear is indulgent,
it said,
there is no time
treachery is everywhere
false comfort
it was urgent, this voice

stop
hold
rise
not this time
not again
never again

they will not win
they will not have us
ever again

there were drumbeats
like explosions
fire rising into the heavens

and there were these demands
from those who had departed

I woke to the sound
of that voice . . .
awaken
now
it's time

that's deep,
Toni says

makes total sense to me,
Sara says

Let's go

We're going to a protest
Toni says

Anji wants to know why
isn't it dangerous?
people get arrested at protests
and sometimes they get hurt

because you have to say something
no matter how dangerous it is,
Rose says,
speak up

you know how you have to give words
to the part of you
that doesn't have words?

we have to give words to people
going through stuff
and they're screaming and shouting

and begging, Toni says

Rose nods,
begging to be heard

Anji looks at the signs,
refugees are people too
science not silence
my body my choice . . .
but what do all these different issues
have to do with us?

yes, Sara says, let's go
she looks at Anji
don't you see?
all of them say please see us
stop hurting us
see our humanity
hear our words

and no one's listening
Anji says, understanding

no one sees them
Toni says,
all of these people, these groups
their bodies and lives
are under attack
just like ours were
and no one is listening
the courts, the cops, the leaders
they're all saying it doesn't matter

these are leaders
who brag publicly about
assaulting women,
Rose adds,
we all heard it
abusers are abusers
whether they're in your house
. . . or in the government,

Sara blows on her sign to dry the paint
they hit you,
she says
hurt your body
then tell you
you are the reason they did it
you are the problem
causing trouble

something deep inside Anji
something that had been tightening
and shifting,
twists now
and ignites

Rose counts on her fingers
if you had behaved better
dressed differently
if you hadn't said what you said
hadn't been so damn pretty . . .

everything they do
is somehow your own fault

Anji's fists clench at her sides
she nods
let's go

Toni and Reshma

Anji watches them
out of the corner of her eye

sometimes
they get ice cream at Rock Slab
and Anji watches them

not because they're girls
but because they have something
she has never known
never seen

they sit together
side by side
not holding hands
not touching
but closer than any two
people sitting apart can be

she can see it
like it's actually there
a current
starting at their sun warmed
shoulders and going down
their arms

just sitting there
on the bench outside of Rock Slab
next to each other

it's almost obscene,
she thinks
to have so much love out here
in public

where everyone can see it
where it makes what you have
look like a whimper

she wants to be close to it
maybe it will rub off on her
if she's close enough

Reshma's mom smiles at them
my two love-birds, she says
she picks them up afterward
and asks Anji if she wants a ride
somewhere

yes, Anji thinks, somewhere
anywhere

just not home

but she shakes her head
and swallows the hard pit
in her throat

getting into that car
with all that love
looks like
it would hurt too much

PART TWO

Leaving

Chapter Thirteen

Saving

It's been a year
and Tuesdays are still
Anji's favorite

that's group night

they haven't added anyone new
because Cathy says
Gina is still there
in spirit

she'll be able to feel our support
Sara says, bringing another chair
this is where her virtual fat ass will sit

Toni laughs
you're just jelly
you wish your ass was that fat

Sara grins
bitch got no idea how lucky she is

Cathy says the girls are making
good progress
and she is so proud of how
they support one another
that healing happens in relationship
because trauma is always in relationship

when Toni looks confused and asks
what about natural disasters
those can be traumatic

Cathy says
absolutely, but people usually
come together during natural disasters
and work together to help the community
get through it
and that is how they heal

no one should have to feel alone,
Rose says
she looks at Gina's chair
you're not alone, she whispers

Anji is writing a lot these days
and the words are coming
more easily now

she feels seen, heard
in a way she never has before
a part of something
larger than herself

like she matters

Assessment

Let's assess, Cathy says,
tugging at her headwrap
she looks like a queen
we've been having sessions now
for a year, she says

Anji nods, a clenching feeling in her belly
you're not going to tell me we have to stop
are you?

Cathy chuckles
no, but I need to fill out these forms
for our organization to continue
receiving funds for services
sometimes that means
a lot of assessment and forms

she looks at Anji with a smile
if we decide we want to extend our
sessions for another year, we can do that

let's do that, Anji says

Cathy's voice goes gentle
next year you turn 18
so we will have to explore
next steps for you

Anji looks at the floor
a slow damp seeping into her skin
I know, she says softly
but that's next year

Cathy places two gentle fingertips
on Anji's shoulder
keep writing,
she says,
keep doing your art

the little flickering flame
in Anji's chest
brightens

it's moving you forward,
Cathy smiles,
it's your magic

Anji nods,
swallowing hard,
yes. finding words
letting her body speak . . .
she would keep doing that

Telling, part 1

Anji is telling her mother

this is what happened

the words are coming out
her heart is clenched
and beating fast

and there is a burning
all throughout her chest

but she keeps going

this is what happened
to me

when I was little

the breathing is hard
shallow
and every muscle is tense

this is what happened to me
when I was little, Mommy

her mother listens
quiet
face very serious

Anji is shocked

she was expecting . . .
something different

but there is no anger
no tears
nothing
just listening

every so often
her mother asks a question
quick
short

what did he look like?
was he one of the younger ones?
did anyone see?

there were two,
Anji says,
an older one and a younger one

her mother's face is stiff
but she nods
for Anji to keep going

Anji tells her everything . . .

Anji

❖

The door would slam
behind Daddy or you,
when you dropped me and Surjit off
at the gurdwara

we would cry
scream
beg
for you

sometimes we would
fall asleep against the door
and they would leave us there

sometimes, when the old lady
was there she would get us
and take us into the kitchen
she would make us popcorn
and we would feel better

but sometimes one of the men
would come and get us

there was one I liked a lot
he was younger and fun
played games with us
joked and laughed and tickled us

I looked forward to seeing him
Surjit liked playing horsie with him

he would take us in the small room
where he slept
and say that he was putting us
down for a nap

and there, on the mattress on the floor
he would do things

he would be on one side of me
and Surjit on the other

once Surjit fell asleep
he would play special games
with me

he would take off my clothes
and I would be naked
and he would put my hands
in places on his body
that I didn't have words for

and he would touch me
in places on my body
that I didn't have words for

there was another man, too
an older one

he would separate me
from the others in the group
and touch me
until it felt like my body
was splintering into
a million pieces

and they liked to scare Surjit
they thought it was funny
when he screamed in terror

you took us there
every morning for almost
two years

you left us there
all day every day
and told us to be good
told us not to make trouble
to do what we were told

and we did, Mom
we were good
we didn't make trouble
we did what we were told

Telling, Part 2

And then they are both quiet

but Anji can feel the tension
in her mother's body
simmering

I never thought it would
happen to you,
she finally says

her voice is trembling
but not from sadness
there is rage there
the same rage that used to
frighten Anji
as a child

except now
it is not directed
at her

it is directed toward the past
maybe a past Anji does not know

her mother's eyes are far away

I thought, she says,
that we kept you safe

I went through these things, too
she says
so many of us did . . .

but they were always in the family
an uncle
a neighbor
friend of the family

Anji's body is still
like when she saw a rabbit that time
afraid to move
and scare it away

who was it,
Anji asks,

her mother doesn't speak
for several long moments

Anji dares not breathe

her mother finally
takes a deep breath
and says,
I can't . . .
it's in the past now
no use in digging it all up

she turns to Anji
your father and I . . .
could never have imagined

and now her mother's face
crumples
but quickly goes back
to her usual stern
solid one

they sometimes sheltered refugees,
she says,
young men fleeing Punjab
in that temple, she says
maybe it was one of the refugees

there were two, Anji says again
a young one and an older one

her mother nods slowly
then it wasn't just the refugees,
she says softly

what difference would it make
Anji asks

her mother presses her lips together
none, she says
it's just hard for me
to imagine
of men who are supposed to . . .

her mother's voice breaks
and she doesn't say any more

they were supposed
to take care of you,
she whispers

her voice is a steel knife
you were supposed to be safe
we trusted them to keep you both safe

in this moment
there is something in her mother
that reminds Anji of Toni
and Sara and Gina and Rose

of all the girls in the group
and she's not sure if her mother
is speaking to her

or if those words are intended
for another little girl
in the past
somewhere only Anji's mother
can see

her mother shakes her head
as if to clear it
why didn't you tell me?
why didn't you say anything?

I didn't want to cause trouble,
Anji whispers,
you and Daddy were already
struggling
we all were

but her mother doesn't hear
her eyes are closed
and her face is lifted

Anji knows her mother
has drifted somewhere else
someplace else
with all the same feelings
as here and now

Chapter Fourteen

Mothering

When Anji was younger
her mother was busy and tired
all the time

no one is listening to me in this life
she would so often say

if she could have picked
her own husband,
she would have picked
someone who took charge
a strong man
no soft-spoken philosopher type

"you're lucky," she'd tell Anji
"you have no idea what my mother was like
she hated me
"no love . . .
there was no love for me anywhere."

Anji's father was always working
and when he wasn't
he was sleeping
her mother would be working too
cooking
cleaning the house

and the kids
always wanting something
needing something

not seeing her
no one truly saw her,
that was what Anji's mother would always say

"you're lucky," she'd tell Anji
"I couldn't go to school,
my mother thought I should stay home
and look after my younger brothers and sisters
but I was smart . . .
I could've been something"

Anji knew, even then
that there was no soft place to land
for her mother
nowhere to pause
nowhere to catch her breath

Anji wanted to help
wanted her mother to know
she saw her
loved her
needed her

"all I need is a shoulder,"
her mother would say

but Anji's was too small

Neesha Meminger

A Bride's value

❖

I would mutter to myself,
her mother says,
when I was doing the dishes
cleaning
cooking

"is this the future
I deserve?"
I would ask the dishes
or the mirror
because I was so alone
all the time

"I perfected myself
made myself everything
everyone wanted me to be,"
I would say to the paneer
simmering in the pot

"I didn't stop making myself
into whatever shape they said
was perfection
until I was a gleaming gem,"

232

I would say to the shirt
I was folding,
"until I was a thread
of unraveled moonlight
that you sold for a bag of rocks"

"that grime I can't rub off my skin,"
I would tell the roti
as I rolled it flat on the counter

she flicks away a lone tear
"everyone said I was lying
when I spoke up about what happened"

"they said it happens
to everyone
all of us
there are always
uncles cousins neighbors

"'you have to be better,'
they said,
"you have to be better
at protecting yourself
better at avoiding it"

then, with a fierceness
that splashes simmering daal
everywhere, she says,
"I would say 'never will I do this to my daughter,
"'she will have a better mother than mine,'"

"'she will not have to scrub her skin
of grime that will not come off.'"

how could I know,
she finishes softly,
that it would happen again
anyway
to my only daughter?

Telling, part 3

Who would believe something
like that? her father says

Anji stares at him
are you saying I'm lying?

she is blown away
by how different
both her parents'
reactions are
both to each other
and to what she thought
they would be

he twists his face scornfully
no one would, he says
you're talking about a temple
a sacred and holy place
men who have taken oaths

those men wouldn't
do something like that
and to a child of all things!

all thoughts vanish from Anji's head
there is something behind
her father's words

she sees wisps of it

he continues,
when men do things like that
the earth opens up
swallows them whole
and demons feed on their insides

Anji stares at him
the door is closing
and this time she isn't
running toward it

she can only stare
at the man
the only man
she'd ever desperately needed…

slamming the door
on his own powerlessness

it didn't happen,
he says

and the slam echoes back
from the past

Neesha Meminger

Vacant

❖

Sometimes their father
would let Anji and Surjit ride on his back

he tossed them into the air
laughing tickling joking
and Anji and Surjit
would scramble back
again and again for more

these are the memories
Anji holds tight to
memories of her father
when he was happy
adoring playful

before endless hours in jobs
with hostile men and
a harsh unwelcoming land
took their toll

one night, something happened
her father ran downstairs
because there was some kind of commotion

it was in the middle of the night
he grabbed a baseball bat

there were young men
with broken beer bottles
on the corner
yelling for them to come out
of their rat shithole
and go back to their caves
where they came from

that night her father
and two other men from the building
went outside

with baseball bats
broom handles rolling pins
whatever they could grab
to protect their families

and there was shouting
and flashing lights outside
and her mother cried

her body shaking, chest heaving
and her father came back inside
hours later

he cried, too
when he thought
everyone was asleep

over time
the years in the new country
changed him
his eyes grew vacant
his gaze pulled backward
into the past
as if trying to pinpoint
just exactly when
everything went wrong

he left, her father who used to let her ride
on his back and throw her in the air
catching her again in his big arms

but his body stayed

he was there
and not there
he grew more and more silent

and their mother shouted
louder and louder
to be heard
to be seen
in a land
where she did not
exist

together, they walked
out into the jaws of the beast
every dark frozen morning
sending prayers up for their children . . .

praying to a god
any god
every god
to keep them safe

Real power

✦

When she told Toni about Kian
Toni asked what was going on

we're talking,
Anji said

he's a couple years older
with super cute dimples
a flop of curly hair on his head
and greenish eyes
he's Persian, I think

Toni grinned
but didn't ask anything more

Kian used to go to their school
so Toni knew him

one day he was visiting the school
and started talking to Anji
as she walked to the bus stop

and now he meets her
every day after school
and they walk home together

today is their first time
hanging out on a weekend

real men protect,
he says
not yell or laugh at people
for being vulnerable

they're talking about power
because that's the topic
in Anji's sociology class this semester
tyrants and authoritarians
and different kinds of power

Kian is helping Anji
think out her paper
which is due at the end of the week

women too,
Anji says softly

he nods
women protect
and nurture children

sometimes men do that, too
she interjects
and sometimes women
can be tyrants

he nods,
it's complicated

he looks up at the sky,
power, like parents and I guess leaders,
is supposed to protect and take care of
people who are vulnerable

but sometimes it does the opposite,
Anji says

that's abuse, he says
stretching an arm across
the back of the bench
behind her shoulders

tiny goose bumps rise
on Anji's skin
she looks up at the sky
to get her breathing back
to normal

there's a day-moon out
ghostly and ethereal

seven generations,
she says,
that's what I read on an IG post

he looks down at her
what about it?

what happened seven generations ago
has led to what's happening now
in our generation

he nods
so what we do now . . .

will affect seven generations
from now,
she finishes

he looks up
at the mystery above
wheeling around

sometimes I feel like we're losing
she says

he's quiet
but she can hear him listening

like what some of the leaders say
and the laws they pass
they feel like abuse

they are the abuse
he says quietly

then after a while he adds
maybe we are losing
but maybe we're not
maybe we're just seeing things
more clearly now

like maybe all of this shit has always been there
maybe all we can do, he says, leaning forward
and brushing her forehead with his lips
is keep trying

she shivers
but doesn't move away
this feels so right
he feels so right

the only way I know
to fight,
she says
is to love
and keep hoping

maybe that's the best way,
he says

what, love?
or hope?

yes, he says

Chapter Fifteen

Waiting

She doesn't know
what he's waiting for

they just keep hanging out
going places
and seeing movies
eating food together

this is not how it was
with Riv

with Riv
they dove right in
sex as soon as possible
as soon as they could
find a place

she didn't love it
but she needed it
the closeness
the warmth
the touch

why haven't you kissed me yet,
she asks

his face flushes pink

he leans on the fence
and stares at the water
flowing below them

every guy Anji has talked to
has moved immediately
on her body

but this
this is weird
maybe scary a little

I want to see you,
he says finally
I want to know things
about you

I like seeing who you are
in different places
with different people

Anji has never seen him
so nervous
she's quiet for a bit
feeling the warmth
of his arm next to her

she looks out at the water

it'll flow into the river
somewhere down the way
and then the ocean
but for now
it's here journeying
always

she gasps and points
look, a snake!
it winds along with the current
just beneath the clear surface

watching it move
Anji realizes
how strong the current is
even if deceptively calm above

he grins
cool!
and a curtain is pulled aside
for just a moment

Anji looks at him,
everything open,
aren't you attracted to me?

surprise skims
across his features

god, yes, he says

he turns and leans one elbow
on the fence
takes her hand in his
kisses the cold tips of her fingers

but I don't have to act on it,
he says
I can control myself

she nods and turns
toward him
she wants reassurance
a guarantee . . . something
a promise, maybe
that there will be no
slammed doors

sex . . . touch
is that immediate intimacy
the only way in that she knows
to that feeling
of being seen
of maybe being loved

she lifts herself up on her toes
brushes her lips against his
her body speaking louder than any words
don't walk out

his kiss is soft
before he gently peels back
I really like you, he says
a lot

he searches her face
like the words are there
scrambled on her skin

Anji wonders if he's
thinking of the girlfriend
he lost

the one who
slit her wrists
and slipped quietly
out of his reach

and maybe his body is saying
things to Anji, too
like, wait
don't drown in your hurt
please
don't let your hurt
pull you away

when he looks back
into her eyes
she circles her arms
around his waist
puts her ear against the thumping
just underneath the surface
of his chest

and they stay like that
for a while
their bodies speaking louder
than anything they could ever say

In her Body

When love is felt
in the body
but the body is the enemy
does that make love the enemy?

some people think
love is recognized
in the heart
but Anji knows it's
in the body

it's there,
written in the body
in an ancient language

a code at once
familiar yet new
a salve
a nutrient

the core and foundation
of everything
every particle of stardust
the whole of the cosmos

but when the body
is the other

when you have been skinned
and left to die
and you don't know
how to fit back in

where do you feel it,
she wonders
how do you find it

Maps

It's luscious
this moment

his hands
mapping
seeking

playing notes on her skin

she's quivering
not with desire
yes with desire but more too

fear longing hope
and that other thing…what's that other thing

he rolls her between his palms
like a ball of cool damp clay

shaping pressing molding
rounding out sharp corners

whispering shiny new skin
over old wounds

he is bringing her to life
from the inside out
something Anji
has never felt before

like when her foot
falls asleep and is waking back up

numb but alive all at once
waking
terrified and elated
tumbling and still

in there somewhere
is a memory
of when she was one
and not two

there is a memory
of a before

and he has found a way
to help her discover it

he touches her
so gently
almost like he didn't
and leaves a trail of
small detonations

Moving

I'm moving out, Mom

everything Anji's taking
is in five boxes
stacked in her room

it took a long time
for Anji to make this decision
and then act on it

but she's hanging on
to a tiny thread inside

the faint voice of truth

howling winds are
whirling around her body
shaking her confidence

this is hard
but staying is hard too

her mother says nothing
only looks at the boxes
and walks away

Anji watches her mother's
silent retreating back
as she goes down the stairs

fight! she wants to yell
tell me to stay!
tell me you're sorry
for never thinking I was pretty
because my skin was too dark

tell me you are on my side
and will publicly say so

that you will always choose me
over men who call me a liar

that you will defend my girlbody
and not tell me to hide it
contort it
shame it
punish it
like you have in the past

but there is nothing
only the click of the front door

and Anji is alone again

Explaining

The boxes are in Reshma's mom's car

Anji goes back inside
to take a last look

in her bedroom,
her mother is sitting
on Anji's bare bed
with the white metal
curlycue frame

remember when we
bought this for you?
she asks

Anji's eyes well up
she nods,
swallowing hard

her mother's eyes are red
she looks at the floor
we made a lot of mistakes,
she says

her voice is wavering
and she pauses for a moment
to take a deep breath

we were trying so hard
to start again
to build back up
after leaving everything behind

she wipes her nose
everything was new
so different
the language
food people weather plants…
and they didn't want us here

her face wants to crumple
but she keeps it steady
Anji can see the shifts
like a fast-motion change of seasons

they let us know how they felt
even the kind ones
that we would always be
outsiders

they let us know
in the banks at work
at your schools
at the post office
in the grocery store . . .

we were frightened
anxious all the time
fighting and alienating
even one another
we couldn't see
you kids

we were afraid for us
for you
afraid we might be sent back
afraid we'd lose you
afraid we couldn't
wouldn't
survive

a small rivulet meanders
from the corner of one eye
to the corner of her mother's mouth
she swipes it away

we had no idea,
she whispers
that the danger
was so much closer

not outside but inside
underneath our noses

Neesha Meminger

Anji stands there
frozen

rivers of emotion
sloshing around
just beneath the surface

for a long time
years, maybe,
as her mother sits
wiping tears from her face

I need to leave,
Anji whispers
I can't stay here anymore

People will talk,
her mother says
what will we tell them?
there will be rumors
questions...

Anji looks at her mother
for a moment
everything colliding inside her

and then quietly
before she bursts
she turns and walks out
of her parents' house
forever

Chapter Sixteen

Holding

Wow, Sara says

that's intense,
Toni agrees

it can be helpful
when a caregiver acknowledges
that there's been abuse
Cathy says

Anji listens
without saying anything
she is so raw

you still moved out,
Rose says, looking down at her hands
I'm proud of you
and honestly?
I would give anything for my mom
to say something to me
anything
to even acknowledge what happened

I had to leave, Anji says
it's like that part of me
that was hurt
can't stay there . . .

Anji tries to find a way to explain

it was being a girl
an embarrassment
at times and a burden at others
it was not being good enough ever

looking after everyone
when no one was looking after me . . .

she searches for a way
to make them understand
that an acknowledgement
at eighteen
is not enough
that it doesn't make her a bad daughter
a bad person

that inside her skin
there is a six-year-old
and ten-year-old
and thirteen-year-old

all doubled over and desperate
for everything
she will never get
no matter how many explanations

Rose reaches out
covers Anji's hand
with her own

I get it,
she says softly

Anji dissolves
and they let her
holding her
cupped in the warmth
of the space they have created
together

Rebuilding

⬦

Anji has moved into a small room
in Reshma's basement apartment
where Reshma lives with Toni
and Reshma's mother lives upstairs

Reshma's parents are divorced
but they are still friends

no, Reshma says, correcting her
not friends
they work together to make sure
I'm okay
but they are definitely not friends

whatever, Anji says
they like each other more than
any other couple I know that are together

in her complete home
with two parents
and two children
a boy and a girl
there was so much sadness

here, at Reshma's
single mom's house
there is light laughter joy
love

broken girls
in broken homes
with broken families

and yet
Anji has never felt
more unbroken

Reshma and Toni are in love
everyone can see it
and Reshma's mom's arms
are always around them
whether she's around or not

now, Anji is under that
arching sunlight

things are thawing
drops seeping into parched earth
buds deep deep down
cracked but frozen
beginning to stir

Anji's mother has been in touch
with Reshma's mom
they've been on the phone
late into the night

and sometimes there is a box
for Anji from home
with sweets her mother has made
or a scarf she stitched
in tears and regret
. . . and love

and sometimes Anji
goes to the house
to sit next to her father
on the sofa
watching anything on tv
or nothing
just sitting

and that's something

and it's enough

Allies

Things are the same,
Surjit says
worse in some ways
better in others

Anji watches the kids
on the playground

she and Surjit are on the swings
at the park by their house
by *his* house
Anji reminds herself

are you mad at me?
she asks
for leaving?

he doesn't answer for a while
just keeps watching the kids

there's one little boy
who keeps filling a pail with sand
and dumping it on his sister's head

yes, he says finally
I am
then he turns to look at her
but I get it

Neesha Meminger

she nods,
I know you do
you are the only one
who was there
the whole time

it sucks,
he says

they sit quietly again
for a bit

do you ever think about it?
the temple, I mean?

he looks at the ground
kicks the rocks at his feet
I try not to,
he says
it was one of the shittiest times
of my life

mine, too
she says

but I don't have a group
or a therapist

you can,
she says

he shakes his head
that's not me
I can't talk about personal
stuff with strangers

she nods
okay, then talk to me
I'm here now
and I was there then
I want to listen

he turns to her
and she sees something
maybe surprise
and then something else
relief? gratitude?

he turns away
clears his throat
but you're not around anymore

we didn't talk when I was around,
she says
we didn't talk in our house

but we can talk now
we can meet here once a week
and we can talk about
whatever you want

Cathy says that when you
shine a light on the hurt
it heals

he looks away
okay,
he says
let's meet here

once a week,
she says

once a week,
he says

then he jumps off his swing
let's go climb the bars,

he takes off
last one there buys me a donut!

oh, hell, no
Anji says
and jumps off her swing

Storms

There is a nor'easter coming
Anji doesn't know what that is
but it's snowing badly outside

she's allowed to walk home by herself
because she's a fifth grader
but Surjit needs to be picked up
because he's only in second grade

she looks down the hall to see
if Mommy has picked him up

he's sitting there alone
on the floor
he sees her
and his eyes light up

she walks to him and says,
"come on, let's go"
the teacher comes out
she knows Anji's his sister
"are you taking him home?"
the teacher asks

everyone else is gone
Anji says yes
the teacher looks uncertain
for a moment
but then lets them go

Neesha Meminger

"what about Mommy," Surjit asks

"maybe she got stuck," Anji tells him
and takes his hand
they head outside
there is a lot of snow
and it is very windy

Anji tightens her grip
on Surjit's hand
pulls his zipper up
so his neck is all covered
and says,
"let's go slow, okay?"

he nods and clings to her hand
they walk out of the schoolyard
and past the first building

"this is not so bad,"
Anji thinks

but when they get to the open area
between the buildings
the wind is very strong
and there is ice on the grassy parts

Anji is scared
the wind is too strong
and she is fighting
to hold on to Surjit's hand

she pulls him to a tree
and shouts,
"hold on to this
until it's not so windy!"

he hugs the tree tight
and Anji hugs him tight
until the wind dies down

then she takes his hand again
and they walk slowly
carefully
on the ice
falling sometimes
but pulling each other up

until the wind
begins to whip around
their faces again

and then they make
their way
to the nearest tree
holding on
Surjit clinging to the tree
and Anji clinging to them both

until the wind stops
howling

like this
they make their way to the hill
now
they have to go down this icy hill
somehow

and across the park
then back up the hill
on the other side

everywhere
there is ice

everywhere
there is howling wind

everywhere
there is snow

there is no one else
in sight

everyone is home
because there is a nor'easter

Anji looks at the vast
icy
windy
snowy
expanse in front of them

and sits down

there are tears running
down her face
mixing with the snow
and wind

she pulls Surjit down
in front of her
between her legs
wraps her arms around him
and scoots both of them
to the top of the hill

"we're going to slide down, okay?"
she shouts into his ear

he nods without looking back at her

they slide down the hill
slowly, not fast
on a sled this would be fun
but in snow pants
it's bumpy
and a little hurty
but they get to the bottom

Anji says
"get on your hands and knees"
and Surjit does what she's doing

they crawl across the valley
where the park is
past the swings
and the teeter-totter
and the empty skating rink

until they are at the bottom of the hill
on the other side

"we're going to climb up, okay?"

he nods
watching her the whole time
mimicking her every move

Anji looks for the unfrozen
patches of grass and pulls herself up
little by little
always looking to make sure
Surjit is climbing too

sometimes he slips
and she has to point him to
an unfrozen patch
so he can find his way up

the wind is sharp
and Anji is not looking
at how much more hill
there is above her

she is only looking at
the next patch of unfrozen grass
and at Surjit
to make sure he is there
with her
climbing

and then they are at the top
they made it
to the top of the hill
together
and they can see their building

now they run
slipping and waiting
for each other
but it's easier now

the wind seems to be quieter
the snow not as thick
they can see home

when they get to their floor
their mother is there
sitting in her coat
in front of the door
in the hallway
her face is gray and long

when she sees them
her eyes glisten
before she closes them
and lifts her face

thank god,
she whispers,

"I went to get you,"
she tells them,
"but you had already left
I couldn't get there in time
because there were no buses
and the bus shelter I was waiting in
collapsed almost on top of me"

"but you're here,"
she says,
"how?"

Anji and Surjit
tell her of their adventure

Surjit's eyes are bright
and he's excited to tell
Mommy all about it

"we slid all the way down the hill,"
he says,
"and climbed up the other hill, Mommy!
in the snow! and ice!"

their mother lifts her face again
and squeezes her eyes,
"thank god,"
she says,
"thank god"

Chapter Seventeen

Investigating

We went to the temple,
her mother says

Anji stops what she's doing
pauses everything –
moving
her heart
her breath

her mother stops too

they stare at each other
like startled gazelles

time drips slowly
one second into the next
until Anji latches onto
one word . . .

why?

something loosens
and her mother's face
becomes a storm

her words come out
like steel
grating against
concrete

to find those men

you . . . and Daddy?
Anji whispers

her mother continues
they're long gone,
they told us
but the main giani there
he sat with us

he said he'd heard of this kind of thing
in other religions
there was a film about it
and a lot of news coverage
about it happening in the
Catholic church, Baptists . . .
she trails off

your dad said,
she begins again,
but not in our religion

the giani said, no
never in ours

Anji is quiet
something is loosening
and falling off of her
like leaves in autumn

her mother notices, maybe
and says gently,
but then your father said,
why not in ours?
men are men, not gods
what makes our men
any different from other men?

she searches Anji's face
your father . . . he said,
when I was a little boy
I was too young to protect my mother
from predators around us
too young and powerless
to protect cousins, friends
girls I loved

so I grew deaf to their voices
stopped listening
to the pain the helplessness
it brought up inside

I let my own child
my little girl
walk into the arms of those men
every morning

I didn't pay attention

tears are streaming down Anji's face
her body has forgotten
how to make words,
thoughts

she is a shadow
in this moment
where an abandoned
six-year-old
standing between a slammed door
and the jaws of a beast

meets a bigger girl
shattered, but not broken

a girl who told

and started stitching back
the scattered
shattered
pieces of her soul

giant waves are crashing
inside

and she is staring at her mother
who is staring back at her
but not seeing her

her mother has become
a raging pillar of fire
her gaze directed somewhere
in the past

and somewhere inside
Anji has the faint thought
that in a different type of family
she might throw her arms
around her mother

might collapse
into an embrace
but this is not that family

other thoughts respond
equally faint:
no, this is not that family
it's not everything
and not enough, maybe

but it's *something*
and for now,
she'll take that

May I find love

❖

His eyes are brown
rimmed with black
shards of sea glass jig-sawed together
into glowing backlit circles

like stained glass windows
in those churches

Anji remembers when
he would wait for his girlfriend
who was in Anji's business class
he would walk his girlfriend
to her next class

and Anji would wonder
if a boy like that
could ever like a girl
like her

at night, she would speak to
the emptiness

the dark is not quiet
it is never empty
it is always alive
gently electric
moving with her and around her

may I find love,
she would say to it

may that epic love
find me

and there was something
in her that just knew
it was finding its way toward her

waiting until everything lined up

waiting for her
to be ready

All wounds heal with a scar

Slower is faster
in healing, Cathy says
let's be in our bodies
for a moment

trauma often makes you leave
your body
because it's too painful

take the clay,
she says, taking her own
feel it, hold it
think of the sensation

what temperature is it?
is it smooth, rough?
close your eyes and
see with your hands

what's happening inside your body?

Anji has a sudden flash
of another pair of hands
long ago, far away
gently mapping the contours
of her face

Cathy instructs the girls
to make a bowl
a *compassionate vessel*

Anji closes her eyes
and pinches and shapes and smoothes
the cold lump in her hands

slowly it warms to her touch
becoming the same temperature
as her body

she's all inside now
working, like a caterpillar
stitching herself together
smoothing the cracks
shaping, hollowing making whole

when she's done
she notices that her vessel
has taken the shape of a heart

now, Cathy says
take more clay and separate it
into three lumps
imbue one with sensation
the second with emotion
and the third with thought

remember, she emphasizes
it's about being here
now
being present

what is a sensation
you can feel
right now?

sculpt it and
when you're ready
place it in your
compassionate vessel
and

when you're ready
do the same with an emotion
sculpt it and place it
in the vessel you've made
and

do the same with a thought
you're having
right now

Anji has to work hard
to separate what is a thought
from what is an emotion
from what is a sensation

everything is just there
inside her body
a body she learned to flee
a body that turned away from itself
cleaving its inside from its outside

slowly, she peels the membranes
thin and filmy like onion skins
sensation, she realizes
is on the body – a feeling
like touch

her sensation
right now is . . .
gas
she can feel it
burbling in her belly

she makes one lump of clay
into bubbles and tubes
and sets it aside

her emotion is not solid
but it is strong
and it has a shape inside her
a color
like a tree, but flat
more like a piece of sea coral
that starts at the very center of her
just below where the solar plexus is

it's throbbing and tender
hurt
red and orange
branching out into her arms
her fingers
and up
condensing into tears
anxiety, she realizes
the emotion is anxiety
she sculpts this, too,
and sets it aside

the third lump
is thought
this is the hardest for her figure out

so many thoughts
that immediately mesh
into emotion and she can't tell
which is which

all that comes up is
don't
don't tell
don't make trouble
don't ask questions
don't be a nuisance

she sculpts a mouth
shaped into a scream
and then she shapes a circle
and places the mouth inside
and then shapes a big red line
that crosses over
the screaming open mouth

pinpricks at the backs of her eyes

she looks at her three sculptures
and wonders how all of those
will fit into that bowl she's made

how could they all fit into that
one small compassionate vessel?

she takes them each gently
and places them carefully
into her bowl

and they fit
there is enough room
in the compassionate vessel
she has created
to hold them

there is enough room in the heart
to hold and heal
all of them

Chapter Eighteen

The making of a fierce girl

Cathy wheels in a hand dolly
with bags of wood
clay nails sandpaper
metal gloves markers
paint string wires

what're we doing,
Anji asks

renovating, Toni says

Cathy laughs
no, she says
let's sit first and I'll explain

they take their seats
always the same ones
in the circle
Cathy Sara Rose Toni Anji
and one empty

they do their centering breaths
close their eyes
and scan their bodies

what are they feeling?
where is it?
what does that feeling
sensation emotion
look like?

they read a poem
or quote or saying
and honor women who've walked
this journey before them

now, Cathy says
I want us to make something
for Gina
to honor her spirit
and our feelings for her

they are all quiet
remembering Gina
wishing she was there
wishing her phone hadn't
been yanked away
all ties to her cut off
no way to get in touch

I would like to invite
each of you, Cathy says
to add your energy
your spirit
and we will create something
together

she leads the girls
inviting them each step
of the way
to build something

I want it to be permanent,
Toni says
and clay isn't permanent

but it's malleable,
Anji says
and warms up to
body temperature

maybe we can add it,
Cathy says
and figure out a way
to make sure it doesn't come off
or change our sculpture in any way

they hammer nails
and there is a platform
and they sand down rough edges

splinters of jagged wood
from trees that once
stood rooted in the earth
firm, knowing they were
exactly where they were meant to be

mother earth,
Rose says
she takes some twigs and branches
cedar and hawthorne
and finds the place on the sculpture
where these belong

Anji shapes clay into features
a face in peace
hands open
serene but fierce

Sara paints
crazy glues string
each follicle of hair
painstakingly placed
precise

it takes a few weeks
to get everything right
sand shredded wood smooth
sculpt the right expression
lay the hair exactly

and they build a prayer
for Gina
a light bridge
connecting her to them

they hold her
in their hands
their hearts
fashioning an invisible series
of chain links between them

so she knows she is never alone,
Sara says, looking at
the fierce girl they've created

Anji walks slowly around
the sculpture
there is a power in it
a sizzling current

what do we do with it,
Toni asks

Cathy smiles
her eyes are misty
you tell me, she says

can we keep her in this room,
Rose asks
I like being close to her
it's like Gina's still here
part of us

she is, Toni says
but this is a monument
she should be outside
for the whole world to see

Anji agrees
everyone should see her
it's Gina and us
all of us
and it's speaking
everyone should hear her

Anji's breath catches in her throat
she looks at the towering sculpture

a warrior woman
fist raised hair flying
serenity on her face
openness in her arms

love's fierce soldier

are you sure
about putting her outside,
Sara asks

Anji can feel her worry
the warrior sculpture feels . . . private
I want to keep her safe
here, with us

but Gina is all about
speaking up, Rose says
looking up at the fierce face

this is Gina's scream,
Anji says
her truth

and ours,
Rose says

Anji nods
our eight-foot
story

Toni looks at Cathy
can we put her
on the center's lawn?

Cathy looks at each of their faces
and gives them a small smile
I'll find out, she says

Toni nods
Anji's right, she says
this is our story
and it should be out there
it's been held inside
too long

it's dangerous,
Sara says
still worried

what isn't,
Rose asks

most of us were hurt when we
were in safe, protected places,
Anji adds
I was in a temple . . .
a sanctuary

her voice trembles
surprising her
but she powers through
being alive is dangerous
so we might as well tell
our stories

there are so many stories out there,
Toni says
and none of them are ours

Rose runs a hand across
smooth wood
sanded down to a silky softness

a statue of Christopher Columbus
is a story, she says
white presidents carved
into a mountainside
that once witnessed sacred songs
and dances of Indigenous peoples . . .
that's a story

paintings of god-the-father
tell a story,
Anji adds
never seeing a
god-the-mother anywhere
in any painting or sculpture
that's a story

yep, Toni says
divine mother, divine father, and holy child
becomes father, son, and holy ghost . . .
that's definitely a story right there

and this, Sara says
eyes shimmering
lips trembling
chin up gazing at the warrior's face
this is our story

Neesha Meminger

she looks at the others
then turns to Cathy
please see if we can put her outside
on the front lawn

Cathy smiles
I will

Rallying

❖

Are you going,
Reshma asks

I don't know . . .
Anji says

I'm definitely going,
Toni says

in the group chat
Rose and Sara said
they weren't going

Toni shrugs
that's their prerogative

my mom's coming with us,
Reshma adds

Anji shifts in her beanbag chair
did you see the link Rose sent though
of those protestors in Portland?
that was scary as hell

but this is a rally,
Reshma says
it's peaceful

yeah, Toni
says bitterly
like that matters
do you think they care

the girls are quiet for a moment
they've all been called things –
unruly, uncooperative, disobedient
wild, provocative

like everything that happened
to them
happened because of them

because of something
they did
said
wore
didn't do
didn't say
didn't wear

Reshma shrugs
we're still going

Powering

Can you believe this,
Toni says,
can you fucking believe this shit?

somebody posted this
on Instagram
it's an actual transcript
word for word

the president of the United States
of America
the leader of the free world
said:

You know, I'm automatically
Attracted to beautiful
I just start kissing them
It's like a magnet
Just kiss
I don't even wait
And when you're a star
They let you do it

You can do anything
Grab 'em by the pussy
You can do anything

that makes me sick,
Sara says,
like I literally wanna barf

me too,
Anji says,
her voice is strained

but that's the point,
Toni says,
this shit is all the way
at the top
not just in our
bathrooms
and bedrooms

I always knew that,
Anji says,
churches temples mosques

courts offices schools,
Rose says

it's all the way
at the top,
Toni says through gritted teeth,

This shit
has got to stop

Chapter Nineteen

Neesha Meminger

Fusing

It is the same energy
as when she was a little girl
in her bedroom

a soft breath
warmth
the faint scent of butter

she doesn't know
if it's a dream
or if she's thinking it

but there's a voice
as clear as if it were
attached to a warm body

it's in Anji's ear
saying things
telling her things

an old woman's voice
when she is awake
or half awake?
Anji is never sure

but the voice is solid
clear
real

Never forget the serpent's spirit

❖

Anji sat up

it was almost dark outside, and she was not sleepy.

something had caught her attention . . .
she didn't know what.

she could hear her mother in the kitchen,
getting things ready, cleaning.
Surjit, her little brother, was asleep on his bed

there was a light at the foot of her bed . . .
where was it coming from?
a glow . . . like around a lamp, or a candle flame
but there was no light and no flame

it moved
like smooth ripples of water

slowly, it took shape
warm copper, coiled at the base
raised, hood fanned

Anji wasn't afraid
the light it emanated felt warm, friendly

"don't be afraid," it seemed to say
it was here to protect her
she was supposed to remember this
to never ever forget

she didn't know how she knew this
but she knew

the snake looked at her for a few long moments
swaying gently

there was the smell of butter . . .
the feeling of a face tilted to sun
eyes closed
warmth, like a breath
warmth, like fingertips tracing her face

and then it began to fade . . .

Anji laid down
before it was gone completely
and went to sleep . . .

the next day
news arrived from the old country

the blind old woman, Anji's great aunt
had passed away during the night

her last words, they said,
were:
bring the girl one last time
tell them I want to see her
just one more time

Neesha Meminger

Warriors and saint-soldiers

You're Sikh, no?
Reshma's mother asks

Sikhs have a history
of being justice warriors
sant-sipahis . . .

we need those now
she says
more than ever

it's a rare man
who challenges other men
especially when they are powerful

men respect strength
even when it is really just tyranny
just fear

sometimes they mistake
their own fear
for respect

instead of facing that fear,
which is really what courage is

that is the Sikh way,
she says,
standing up to tyranny
fighting the good fight

but all men are afraid
in this manworld
because they were once children

children who faced tyrants
under the guise of grown men

sometimes fathers
uncles grandfathers priests
fathergods

and sometimes that fear
leads them to defend the tyrant
to silence the vulnerable

blame the powerless
laugh at what they see
as weakness

they'd rather be
the one hurting
than the one hurt

they come face to face with
their own powerlessness
and it reminds them of being children
and that's scary
in the shadow of violence

and the only power
they saw was abuse
of power

so, easier to yell at
the vulnerable
and smash the vulnerability
in your own self

but true courage
true justice warriors
face fear even if their heart
pounds furiously
in their chests

they speak
say wrong is wrong
under threat
of violence or
persecution

that's what Reshma's mom says
before going off to bed
just to Anji because Reshma went out

that night, Anji lies in bed
damp pillow beneath her cheek

she knows
there was a part of her father
who believed her
and a part that wanted to believe
these things
don't happen

he had
a giant beast
of his own
that would swallow him whole

she needs him
to believe her
even if he never truly can

somewhere
in a deep fissure
buried under the weight of time

Neesha Meminger

there is a little girl
waiting for her father
to come back

to structure a life
around keeping her safe
a tender, wavering flame

waiting

life is resilient
but fragile
and hope,
even more so

hope
once extinguished
means
life is not far behind

patriarchy eats its young

Anji looks at the walls
of the small room
she now lives in

home

this room inside Reshma's house
her mom upstairs
a phantom dad
who sends money

here, Anji is alone
but safe
healing and hurting
constantly fleeing
and coming home

Anji misses everything
she never had

fresh tears on the pillow
under her temples
wending their way
through the strands of her hair

she misses her home
with her mother
Surjit
her father
but that home was jagged
sharp points and prickly

how can you miss
something
you never had?

maybe because
you had everything once

when you were born
with everything
you were everything

that, Anji thinks,
is what we miss
even if it lives nowhere
but in our body's
memories

Chapter Twenty

Moving from a place of love

What would happen if we moved
from a place of love and not fear . . . ?
Sara asked one time

because that is truth
god is truth
and god is love

and if we all moved from love
not fear
we would engage that magic
we are meant to be

the magic our ancestors knew
when they mapped the stars

when they knew you
would walk this earth
the same earth
they walked

under the same stars
the same moon
the same sun

we have forgotten love
forgotten that when we move
from love we soar

all of us, together

What do you like about me?

❖

I like feminine,
he says

what's feminine,
Anji asks

he twirls a piece of her hair
thoughtfully before saying,
strength

what's that quote
you showed me on IG?
something about men
are excited by women

Anji pulls out her phone,
'Strong women intimidate boys
and excite men,'

yeah, that's the one
who said that

she shrugs
Coco Chanel?
Eleanor Roosevelt?

you're strong,
he says
but in this vulnerable way
and you trust
even with all the shit
you've been through

and that trust and that
openness and vulnerability
is your strength

and then you wrap
this kind of love
around it all
in a way that just feels . . .
he trails off

you know what I like?
Anji asks

he shakes his head
and lightly traces
her jawline up to
her earlobe and then
begins the detailed task
of tracing the contours
of her ear

masculine, she says
her voice is raspy
I love masculine
no matter what
package it comes in

he stops and pulls back
to look at her face
like…girls, too?
like your friend Reshma?

maybe, she says
why not?
Toni feels masculine
to me
but feminine too
and Reshma feels feminine
but masculine too

his face looks uncertain
all of a sudden

she moves closer
it's like water, maybe
she says
it moves
changes shape and form
but still always love
and still always desire

there's a strong pull for me
in the masculine
how I define it

and the desire in me
doesn't care about how
it's expressed or who
expresses it
I just move toward it
and I . . . I just trust that pull

she places a hand
against his face
cupping one side
and stands on her toes
to brush a soft kiss
against his warm neck

how do you define it, then
masculine,
he asks

she's thoughtful
for a moment

strong, she says
but in a different way . . .
more like gentle-strong

like your dad?

she nods,
but stands up to other guys
even if he's scared
you know?

he nods and pulls her in
sets his chin
on top of her head
he smells like soap and cinnamon

he leans back
and looks into her eyes
you know what I read today?
that the word husband
actually means *to cultivate*

hmm, Anji says
like animal husbandry

yeah, he says
one corner of his mouth tilts up
into a smile,
it's to grow something
like a farmer

she tightens her arms
around him
I think that's what love
should be,
we should all husband
each other

he laughs
and Anji puts her ear
against his chest again

to hear that laughter
vibrating there
near his heart

How do you do it?

How can you be open
to me
here
like this,
he asks

she lifts herself up
on an elbow,
what do you mean?

some of the things
you've told me . . .
like what happened
when you were little

he doesn't say anything for a minute

neither does she
her chest feels tight
like there is no air

he cups her face
kisses her lips
so soft like flower petals

What Girls Know

I just don't know
if I could be like you
after some of those things
if they'd happened to me

she's quiet for a while
waiting for the breath
in her body to
go back to the way
it knows to move

in and down the center
hold
out and up the center

then she looks into his eyes
but this time
she doesn't want to flit away

she wants
so desperately
for him to see

she falls quiet
for a while,
her eyes on the grass between them

and he doesn't say anything,
waiting

finally, she
looks back into his eyes,
it should be a mystery,
she says

her eyes fill
but she is determined
to find the words
and make him see

sex should be
like honoring this great
mystery
of desire
of wanting
honoring

it's how the life force
births itself

it should bring you
to your knees
in reverence

you should know
without a doubt
that you are in the arms
of something divine

it should be like a prayer,
she says
but I didn't get that
so many of us don't get that

he furrows his brow
but he's still,
listening

that's why I don't understand,
he says finally,
how you can bear
to let anyone touch you
at all

she inhales and thinks about that,
when an eighteen-wheeler
is coming at you,
she says,
you flee

Neesha Meminger

it is the smart thing
to do
you leave your body and wait
for it to be over

but at some point
later
you have to go back
to get that
crumpled heap
on the floor

and then
the love hurts
more than when
that truck
slammed into you

because now
you're feeling it

now
you're waking up

fighting to come back
to this body
abandoned

and you're plucking love
in fistfuls
from wherever you find it

and draping it around
your shoulders

and gasping for
that sweet cool air
when you break the surface

that's what you are,
she says,
my sweet cool air

his voice cracks
but why,
he says,
what makes you
want to open up
to *me*?

her eyes rest gently
on his face,
girls go through
our entire lives,
she says,
fending off guys

men uncles strangers
fathers husbands bosses

every single day

we avoid eye contact
swat away groping hands
watch hear understand
something offensive
on tv the news online on a billboard

every single day
there is at least one thing
that reminds us
that we have to always
be vigilant
awake
alert

we are walking
fortresses

ready and prepared
in all our different ways
for whatever might come

and you,
she says,
moving closer

you have never
made a single move
without asking first

you ask
you always ask

and you don't move
until you know for sure

and even then
you check again

how did you get like that,
she asks

there is a small smile
playing on her lips now

he smiles too,
lots of practice
getting rejected

enthusiastic consent
is what they called it in health class
she says,

I can see now
how hot it is
to be with someone
who won't touch me
without my enthusiastic consent

hot, she teases,
and frustrating

laughter dances
in his eyes,
then maybe you have to be
more enthusiastic

Chapter Twenty-One

Neesha Meminger

Can you get me?

❖

I'm in jail

it's Surjit

calling her

at midnight

it takes her a few minutes
to understand

I was arrested,
he says

there is urgency
in his voice

can you come?
he asks

of course

of course

The other side of glass

He was in the wrong place
at the wrong time,
Surjit's friend says
in his texts to her

Kian says
I'll take you

the texts continue
we were in the wrong
part of town

and there were
stolen goods
in the truck

Surjit just happened
to be driving
we never meant to include him

I stayed back
because someone needed
to be at the house . . .

Anji texts back,
can't talk about this now
and puts her phone on
do not disturb

I'm going in alone,
she says to Kian

are you sure?

she nods
she knows Surjit
will not want him there
a stranger

there are uniforms
and bright lights inside
so much light amidst so much
darkness
so bright
and so cold

she is led to a room
and asked to wait
and then she is taken to another room
with other people
and little sectioned cubicles

and then Surjit
is on the other side
of the glass partition

he sits down at the cubicle
she has been led to
and takes the phone on his side
he points to the phone next to her

she picks it up

this is the only way
she can talk to her little brother

on a phone
when he's right
in front of her
but she can't
touch him

no warmth

just look at him
looking at her
both of them
holding a cold, stupid phone

with thick glass between them

don't tell mom and dad,
he says
please?

she closes her eyes
for a moment
she knows why
but asks

they're gonna get
mad at me,
he says
and it's gonna be
like I did this to them

no, she says
you did this
to you

something flashes in his eyes
and his voice gets
really low

you don't think,
he says
that they crawl
through brown neighborhoods
looking for guys like me?

you don't think they saw me
and saw every brown
criminal on tv
in the news
in movies?

this is not the time
to cry
and so she doesn't
but she knows
that there is so much
she doesn't know

that this world eats boys
differently than it eats girls
and Surjit is looking for
his warmth, too

okay, she says
I won't tell them

she touches the glass
with three fingertips
and the print stays there
on the cold hard thick glass
after she moves them

don't worry,
she whispers into the phone
we'll figure this out too

Breaking

What is mental illness
and how is it diagnosed

let's say a man
when he was a boy
was afraid all the time

afraid of yellings
and beatings
afraid of seeing
his mother beaten
of bloodshed in the streets

afraid of red stained sickles
against stretched brown necks
bodies lying in the wheat when it was gold
dancing tall in the dipping sun

let's say that boy
heard his worthlessness
rebounding in the dark

when he was trying to sleep
but never could

and let's say
he lost his mother
one day she stepped onto a bus
to go to the big city
one beautiful cloudless day
and never came back

what if he and his brothers
combed every city in the province
with a black and white photo
of their mother

and no one
not one person
had seen her

and let's say this man
moved across an ocean
to another tongue
another climate
another landscape

with a hopeless and
devastated wife
and two small children
two children who
desperately needed his protection

let's say his first
for real home
in this new land
was burned black
on the inside

all the walls charred
black paint left untouched
pakis go home

and let's say the job
at the factory
he was so grateful for
put him in a cafeteria
with men

who thought the country
only had room for one group
immigrants

thought it funny
to dump his lunch
in the trash
replace it with feces

but it was okay
he could handle
even that

because he was providing
for his kids who were
safe in a temple
watched over in
a house of god

what is mental illness
and how is it diagnosed

is it something that breaks
in the mind
or does it break
in the heart

does it leave
your eyes vacant
and make the past
a numb canvas

memories vanishing
like raindrops
on hot concrete

Cracking

She went to pick up Surjit
at the jail

they moved you,
she says,
without telling anyone
not me, not the social worker

his face is blank
that's what they do

she's shaking
she yells,
they put you in an adult prison

he keeps looking out
of the window
seeing something
Anji can't

maybe something
no one can

when she'd picked him up
in the car she borrowed
Surjit was holding his jeans up
to keep them from falling down

his breath smelled
from a distance
he hadn't washed in days

what happened to your belt
she asked
she knew they probably took it
when they put him in that place

they moved me,
he said,
still looking out

I never got my stuff back

she takes him
to her room
in Reshma's house
to clean up

when he comes out of the shower
he says,
I can't stay in that house
with mom and dad

she looks at the backs of her hands
on the table
a long time ago
these hands were bigger
than his

remember that story,
she says,
mom used to tell us

the one about the lovers
sohni mahival
and how she used to cross
the river using a pot
to keep her afloat

he nods
yeah, and one time someone switched the pot

she nods,
someone jealous of the lovers
switched the pot to one that hadn't been baked
and when sohni crossed with it

she drowned,
he finishes

our home was like
this sort of gorgeous piece
of pottery,
she says quietly,
it looked real

but when you tried
to hold on to it
it would slip away
and we'd end up with
handfuls of soggy clay

drowning,
he says

they're both quiet
for a long minute

in that tiny cell,
he says,
I slept on the floor
two guys already had
the bunks
so I slept by the toilet

little pieces of Anji's
heart crumble off
and fly away

disappearing like
dandelion wishes

you can stay here,
she says
I haven't asked Reshma's mom
but I'm sure it'll be okay
and if she says no
we'll find something else

something opens in his eyes

for the first time
since she brought him back
she can see
the Surjit she knows
has always known
for his whole life

the Surjit that was at the temple
with her when their father left

the Surjit that was at home
when their mother yelled
and outside with her when their
apartment burned

at school with her when the kids
were shouting at their backs

she sees that Surjit again
for an instant

it's okay,
he says
no one would rent to us
and you got a good thing here
he waves to her small room
in Reshma's mom's basement

I'll go back,
he says
it's okay
I'll wait til I'm 18
like you did

you can come here
anytime,
she says

her voice catches
in her throat
even if I'm not here
you can come over
if you need to

she takes his hand
he's hard and cold
and frozen

she takes his hand
and doesn't let go

Chapter Twenty-Two

Anchors

An anchor
that's what her mother had always been
her anchor

the cord always attached
like a chain
she was safety
she was home

her English teacher
once said that the Chinese
character for home
was a mother
and a child

what to do when
home and safety
are also frightening
and foreign

what to do when the sacred
is also the site of desecration

there, on that hallowed ground
so holy that shoes must be removed
heads covered, bowed in reverence

what to do when safety
and holy and home
become the jaws of a beast

from which you must flee
but there is nowhere to go
no one to save you at all

then

you become the spider
and you locate the anchor within
the anchor that was always there

your own anchor

there is no chain
only a cord
tied only to you

and then you weave

because it is there
all of it
within you

home

the sacred and the holy
it is there
right there

in your belly
two fingers below your bellybutton
your center

like the spider carrying
everything she needs
for home
safety
in her belly

and you weave your silk
your own silk
from your body
creating shimmering threads
into strands

that will support you
hold you
cradle you

in a magnificent
glittering home
that you made
from your own body

Embers

The body knows a lie
before you do
it rejects the lie so thoroughly
that it begins the process of removing it
immediately

the body does precisely
what it was designed to do
it ousts the invader

and if you fight it
fight to keep the lie

insist the lie is true

the body will fight you
because then you are
the invader

the body is truth
ask it
what lie has wormed its way in?

and it will tell you

Lies outside

There are hateful disgusting words
spray-painted
all over the fierce girl sculpture

someone in the cover of night
a coward
when we weren't looking
wrapped a rope around her neck
and battered a hole right through her center
between her legs

she was supposed to be safe,
Sara sobs
you said she was going to be okay

she was on center property,
Cathy whispers
she was supposed to be safe

I was supposed to be safe, too
Anji says
her voice is flat
in a temple
a house of god

we all were,
Toni says
we were at home
with people we were supposed
to trust

yes,
Cathy says
her voice is hard
like a knife
we are supposed to be safe

it is our birthright

Walking and honoring

How do we go on
when we are paralyzed
with rage
with fear
terrorized

how do we will one foot
in front of the one that has stalled
that has frozen
in time
in trauma
a death

where do we how do we
create light
when all around us has dimmed
a silent scream in the dark
oxygen blotted out
dying without death

where do we find hope?

we create,
Cathy says

her voice is a pillar of fire

as long as there is breath
in our bodies, we create

she reminds us there are women
who used to be with us
and with us no more

women whose lives were cut too short
women and children who never got as far
as we have

she reminds us that we are here
for them, too

so lift your foot,
she says through clenched teeth,
the one that won't move

lift it for them

because when you walk
you honor them
you sing their songs

you continue their fight
you don't let them die
in vain

if you are still here
you are here for a reason
so sing, goddammit

lift that foot
and put it ahead of the other
walk

and fight
and sing
and dance

and heal

they will live on
through your song
your struggle

you are
their
hope

Eve

The stories they tell us,
Cathy says,
the ones we hear when
we're just learning
our first words
shape who we become

and then we have to
spend the rest of our lives
unlearning them
and rewiring our brains
to love ourselves
again

you have to think
about the stories we learn

the very first ones
we're told

for me it was fairy tales,
Rose says

especially those,
Toni says

Flames

I need to read it,
Surjit says,
like out loud

to the air in the room
to the sky the grass the walls
I don't care

I just need to say it
like free the words
or something

sometimes I feel like
I want to crawl
out of my skin

Anji nods,
her eyes stinging
she knows what he means

but this time
this space
is for his words
not hers
so she waits

I wrote this thing,
he says,
because I needed to
I was sitting there
and it just came out
on this napkin

can I read it to you?
can you listen?

of course,
Anji whispers,
always

he starts reading,
the world is burning
in the hands of a madman

and hate has
come out
from under its hood

an endless pit
emptiness
is swallowing the poor

this planet
the earth
everything good

is burning
like something dying
so something else can live

this is what happens when
you kill half of yourself
and have to come alive again

birth and death
ride together

black and white stallions
on a chariot

Malcolm said,
no one can give you freedom
you have to take it

he said,
pass the truth
to the next generation

Martin said,
none of us are free
until all of us are free

Baldwin said,
it was the floods last time
and the fire next time

Surjit stops here
for a long moment
and inhales a deep shaky breath

next time is now,
he says when he begins again

the world is reaching up
in flames

his voice breaks
and he abruptly shrinks back
into himself

Anji is at his side
in a flash
cocooning him

until he can
catch his breath
until he can breathe again

the cool air going
into his lungs
keeping his body warm

his voice still vibrating
in the air of the room

Chapter Twenty-Three

A rally

✦

The rally is an ocean of people
as far down the avenue as you can see
covering the entire park

all kinds of people
on foot in wheelchairs
on motorcycles on bikes
with flags signs whistles drums

Anji has never seen anything like it

there are signs about everything
unions
#metoo
black lives matter
idle no more

the fierce girl
carefully mended
is on the center stage
where everyone can see

Reshma's mom got everyone
#metoo and #resist signs

Kian is at Anji's side
wearing a sign that says
the time is now #riseup

he hands Surjit a #resist sign

Surjit grasps it firmly
eyes aflame
and raises his other hand
in a fist full of hope

at one point
in the middle of it all
Anji stands listening to the drums
beating around her
feeling them through the earth

the chants of strangers
she is falling in love with
before her and behind her

and for a long moment
it all falls away
and there is a warmth
beaming down on her
a buttery glow

these are uncertain times
and there are fires burning
everywhere

mother earth and mother nature
pleading for justice
demanding change

and all around her
fists are raised
in hope and fury

and Anji realizes this is
so big and she is so small
but so important

her voice
however broken
however shaky
is needed

she raises her sign
#religiontoo
#metoo
and adds her voice
to the rising chorus

Other ways

❖

They are dissolving the program,
Cathy says,
there is no funding

that's bullshit,
Rose says,
there's always money
for the people at the top

funding always gets cut
when it's for women or girls
or poor people

Toni's face is red
but she's sitting perfectly still
yep, she says,
the CEOs always get their bonuses

Anji can't tell
if she's sad or angry

Cathy is quiet
after a moment she says,
we are trying to find other ways

isn't that the story of our lives,
Sara says,
we are always trying to find
other ways
I'm fucking tired
of finding other ways

loving ourselves is a revolutionary act,
Anji says,
that's what Audre Lorde told us
they don't want us to love ourselves

no one says anything
for a moment

but we do anyway,
Rose says finally,
we live
we fucking live

Angels of light

Sometimes I feel hopeless, Anji says

Toni looks out over the lake
I know, she says
remember that session we had on hope?

Anji nods,
it didn't help

hot fat tears
slide down her cheeks

sometimes, she says,
it feels like god
forgot me

like . . . how could a god
that loves us
let things like that happen
to little girls?

Toni fishes around in her backpack
and comes up with a crumpled napkin
and hands it to Anji

for several moments they're both quiet
watching the fingernail moon
dance on the small waves

Toni's not good at hugging
or touching

and right now
Anji could use . . . something

Toni draws in a deep breath
and says softly,
you know when caterpillars
are turning into butterflies . . .

they make a cocoon
and then they're in it
in that cocoon
in the dark
and they don't know anything else

that's their whole entire world
and they basically turn into this soup
of caterpillar parts

they have to break everything up
in there, in that cocoon
and reassemble themselves

Anji's tears are drying on her skin
she glances at Toni and nods

Toni is still looking at the moon
on the water
breaking and reforming
and breaking again

the thing is, Toni says,
her voice small on the breeze
gentle, like the moonlight

they have all the butterfly parts
in there, in the cocoon
they don't go out and get new parts

everything they need to turn into
little flying angels, they have
when they're caterpillars
crawling on the ground
with the worms

and when they're in there
in that caterpillar soup
they don't know what they're
going to become

they don't even know
what's pushing them
to do this thing

glue together whatever it is
they don't know
that they're gluing
together

but something pushes them
and they don't know
that there's a world outside
of their little
cocoon

they're just working nonstop
in the dark
to rebuild their dissolved bodies

she falls silent for a long minute

why don't they teach you that?
Anji says quietly,
it's more useful than algebra

Toni grins,
I had a butterfly garden
when I was little, she says

I looked up everything I could
about butterflies

she pauses, and then adds
that was where I found hope

Anji stares out at a rock
jutting just above the surface
of the water
small waves lapping gently over
its jagged corners

I wonder, she says,
if that caterpillar feels alone
and forgotten in that cocoon . . .
like, what is all this for,
and if maybe it should just give up . . .

Toni turns to her and gives her a small
thoughtful smile,
none of them ever did, she says
in my butterfly garden
none of them ever gave up

all the while they were working away,
she says,
there was this force outside
knowing that the caterpillar
would emerge

into this dazzling and brilliant
spark of colored light
that would float and soar
far higher than it ever
could have known was possible

Anji drops her head onto Toni's shoulder
and allows her eyes to flutter closed

Toni doesn't move
just lets Anji rest her head

you know, Anji says,
you might not be good
at hugging or touching
but your words are like
soft hope filled blankets

Skin

I want something to show
how I've changed, Anji says,

I thought that's what you were
writing your book for,
he says

It is, she nods,
but that's to show what's different inside
I want something that shows
how I've changed on the outside

I feel like I'm walking through a gate
shedding a skin and coming out new
and I need to honor that

he strokes her forearm
with one hand
the other arm
around her shoulders

did you know, she asks,
that snakes go blind while they're shedding
their skin?

he shakes his head

they need to focus, she says,
they're moving their old insides
into a new outside

and when they're done
their old skin looks like
a complete version of their old self

but they've moved on
bright and shiny and new
I looked it up

it's probably painful, he says

and now they are at the tattoo place
Anji shows the artist
the image Kian drew for her

the artist who says his name is Oz
looks thoughtful
then makes a few adjustments and
holds it back up for her

a smile spreads across her face
that's it, she says
her eyes are dancing

Kian cups her chin
locking his eyes with hers

that's the one?

she's trembling
yes, she says, and turns to Oz.

do it

why a cobra, Oz asks,
as he shaves her forearm
and swabs the area with alcohol

I had a vision of one
a long time ago, she says

he nods, not missing a beat
like a kind of guiding light, he says
and looks up

in my culture, he says,
we believe
your guiding light reveals itself
to you early in life

then he nods to himself
and gets to work

there is a rainbow flag behind him
with a circle overlaying the rainbow
a circle of red black white and yellow

there is no talk for a bit
and Anji thinks butterflies
might have been Toni's guiding light

a couple of minutes
into the tattooing
Anji feels like she's going to pass out

Kian gets a cool damp paper towel
and presses it to her forehead

totally normal,
Oz says,
you need sugar

he hands her a raspberry lollipop
and waits

Anji closes her eyes
takes a deep breath
and gives him a slight nod

she's ready.

About the Author

Neesha Meminger was born in a village in Punjab, India. She grew up in Toronto, Canada, lived for 25 years in New York City, and now divides her time between NYC and Toronto.

Neesha's first novel, *Shine, Coconut Moon*, made the Smithsonian's list of Notable Books for Children in its debut year and was listed on the New York Public Library's Stuff for the Teen Age–Top 100 Books for Teens. The book was also nominated for the American Library Association's Best Books for Young Adults. Her second novel, *Jazz In Love*, was picked by the Pennsylvania School Librarians' Association for their top 40 selections for young adults and was a recommended summer read by *Bookslut*. Both *Shine, Coconut Moon* and *Jazz In Love* were nominated for the online CYBILS award. The Canadian Children's Book News had this to say about Neesha's third novel for Young Adults, *Into the Wise Dark*, "[T]he novel's lyrical rhythms give the reader a sense of history, ancient Goddess spirituality and the emotional turmoil of Pammi's experience. Inspired by South Asian mysticism and history . . . this rich tapestry of experience [shows] the multicultural reality of our modern world."

What Girls Know is Neesha's fourth book. Learn more about Neesha online at NeeshaMeminger.com.

Twitter/IG: @NeeshaMem
On Facebook as Neesha Meminger

Also by Neesha Meminger

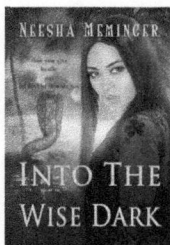

"Into the Wise Dark describe[s] the passion, fear, and all-encompassing joy of first love, without the clichés . . . [T]he novel's lyrical rhythms give the reader a sense of history, ancient Goddess spirituality and the emotional turmoil of Pammi's experience. Inspired by South Asian mysticism and history . . . this rich tapestry of experience [shows] the multicultural reality of our modern world.

—CANADIAN CHILDREN'S BOOK NEWS

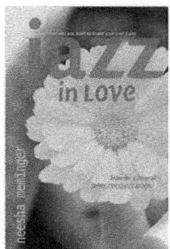

"What made Jazz in Love so enjoyable... was the narration, which reminded me a bit of Meg Cabot both in its humor and how Jazz remained endearing even when you know she's making a mistake."

—KIRKUS

"A beautiful and sensitive portrait of a young woman's journey from self-absorbed naiveté to selfless, unified awareness."

—SCHOOL LIBRARY JOURNAL

"An enjoyable, difficult-to-put-down book."

—VOYA

www.ingramcontent.com/pod-product-compliance
Lightning Source LLC
Chambersburg PA
CBHW032051090426
42744CB00005B/172